# SQUARE PEG

Learn to Stand Up and Be a Square Peg

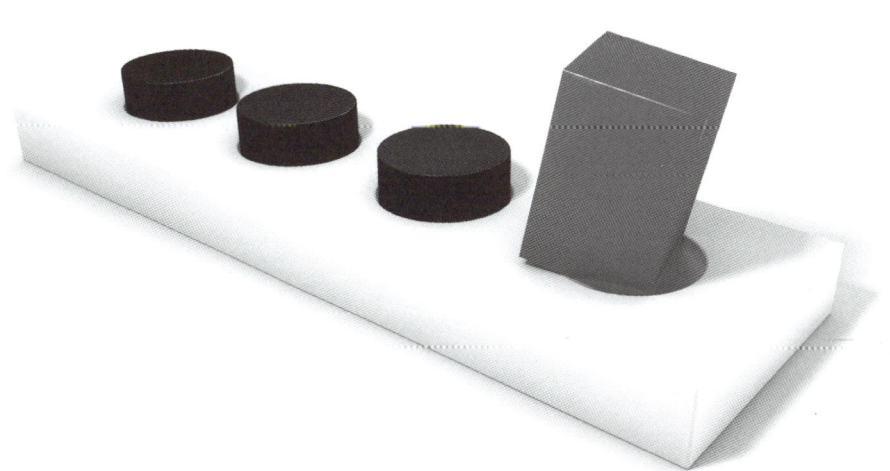

## CHERYL WYLLER

## Square Peg
### Learn to Stand Up and Be a Square Peg

Copyright © 2024 by Cheryl Wyller

Published by Book Ripple
www.BookRipple.com

All rights reserved. No part of this book may be reproduced or transmitted in any form or by any means, electronic or mechanical, including photocopying and recording, or by an information storage and retrieval system, without permission in writing from the author.

ISBN: 978-1-959508-18-2
Printed in the United States of America

To contact the author, go to:
www.educ8collabor8.com

# PREFACE

This book was written out of a deep passion for reading, learning, and sharing the importance of social-emotional support. I focused on bullying because I feel it's a problem that's starting in elementary school. We need to help children understand what they can do.

This book does not focus on the bully; it focuses on the bystander.

Things would change if more kids stood up for the victims and made the bullies feel that they were doing something wrong. Things would change if the bullies weren't glorified with crowds, videos, and praise.

Another goal is to assist anyone working with a child on their reading comprehension skills. I want to continue to help others be equipped with the appropriate information and specialized questions to be able to increase the student's reading comprehension, not just check for engagement with the book. That is why I included reading comprehension content at the end of the story.

I would love to have this book used in multiple areas: classrooms, libraries, book clubs, and homes. I would love to work with people who are using this book as a tool for multiple platforms. What better way to get children to discuss hard issues while building their reading skills than making it a part of their education?

# DEDICATION

To my amazing children who have been my guinea pigs and focus group for all topics related to bullying, being kind, and reading comprehension since early elementary school. Because of you both, I know talking about the hard topics early is effective and builds character. Because of you both, the world is a better place.

To my husband, thank you for supporting me on my new adventure. I appreciate you and am excited to have you on this new journey with me. C4

# INTRODUCTION

# DAY BEFORE SIXTH GRADE

I can remember everything I learned in elementary school like it was yesterday. Technically, I was there less than three months ago, but still.

One of my favorite games as a kid was that wooden bench, the one with the hammer and the different-shaped pegs. There were squares, circles, and triangles. I remember I would get so frustrated when one didn't go where I wanted it to go. I would just bang and bang and bang the peg, making it fit where it wasn't supposed to go.

One time I was determined to get the peg to fit. I went into my dad's toolbox and got out a real hammer. I hit the square peg as hard as I could. I got the square peg into that circle hole, but the peg was in pieces. It didn't seem worth it in the end. I had ruined the square peg, and I had liked that one most of all.

...

In kindergarten, I was playing with the wooden bench game, and the teacher came over to watch me. She told me to never put a square peg in a round hole.

"Don't put things where they don't belong," Mrs. Philips said sternly, "everything has its own place."

"I enjoy putting them in different spots. I think it's fun." I looked at Mrs. Philips, waiting for her to tell me it was ok. I was hoping she would understand that since I liked it, it would be no big deal.

"Everything has its place. A square peg does not belong in a round hole," Mrs. Philips announced before she walked away. I remember watching her leave and feeling like something in me had changed. She just altered something I had always believed in, something I always thought was okay. I wondered if this went for everything.

I got home, got a Sharpie, and opened my closet door. In big letters behind the door, I wrote:

    LESSON LEARNED

    1.   NEVER PUT A SQUARE PEG IN A ROUND HOLE

# CHAPTER 1

# REMEMBERING FIRST GRADE

In 1st grade, I dropped a box of 100 crayons in a hallway full of kids. I was embarrassed and rattled. A girl that I had just met that day stopped walking and helped me pick up all my crayons. I was so grateful that someone was nice to me. It meant a lot.

The next day I saw someone spill their lunch tray when they were walking back to their seats in the lunchroom. Kids giggled at the little boy. I felt bad for him. I put down my lunch box and helped him clean up his mess. It made me feel good to pay it forward. I began to understand the true meaning of what my parents always told us. It felt good to be kind.

I didn't tell my parents that they were right, but I did go home that day and get a Sharpie. I went to my closet door and opened it. I looked behind my door. First, I added an S behind the word LESSON. I had a feeling I'd be learning a few more. Then I added my second lesson.

LESSONS LEARNED

1. NEVER PUT A SQUARE PEG IN A ROUND HOLE

2. ALWAYS BE KIND

# CHAPTER 2

# SECOND GRADE HAD A HARD LESSON TO LEARN

It's amazing how much trouble you can get into in second grade. I was coloring a picture that was due at the end of the day. I was proud of my work. I used different colors, I made sure I colored inside the lines, and I even tried to make it look realistic. I proudly walked up to the teacher's desk to hand in my picture. As I looked down, I saw my friend Anna's paper. Hers was prettier and brighter. I was jealous.

I made a quick decision. I glanced around the classroom to make sure no one was looking at me. I quickly erased her name and wrote mine. I then wrote Anna's name on my paper and put them both in the box on the teacher's desk. I walked back to my desk.

The school day wasn't even over before the teacher called me back up to her desk. I didn't know if I was going to get told how beautiful my picture was or if I was about to get in trouble. I decided to walk up to the teacher's desk confident that I was about to be told my picture was great.

Nope, I got in trouble. Mrs. Hinders had both pictures on her desk. She asked me what happened and quietly waited for my response. I had a split second to make the right decision. I panicked.

"I don't know," I whispered.

"Are you sure?" Mrs. Hinders just stared at me. I'm not even sure she blinked. In my mind, she was breathing fire and shooting lasers out of her eyes at me, waiting for me to tell the truth. It was nothing that exciting, though. She just stared at me, waiting for me to say more.

"Well," I stuttered, "my name is on that one." Maybe that would be enough information to make her happy. As I looked closer, I could still see Anna's name where I had written mine. Under my breath, I huffed, "Well, that didn't work so well."

"LilyAnn, we're going to have to call home and talk to your parents. What do you think we should tell them?" I remember thinking that I could make up a believable story. I thought I could say Anna wanted my paper instead, so we traded.

I looked down at the pictures and then twisted my hands into pretzels. "We'll tell them the truth. I erased Anna's name because I thought her picture was better."

We called home. I got in trouble for cheating, lying, and being dishonest to my friend Anna. However, since I told the teacher the truth, I was still able to go to my friend's birthday party that weekend. I had been looking forward to that for a whole month.

When I learned about the compromise for telling the truth, I ran right into my bedroom. With a Sharpie in my hand, I opened my closet door and wrote the new lesson I had learned.

LESSONS LEARNED

1. NEVER PUT A SQUARE PEG IN A ROUND HOLE

2. ALWAYS BE KIND

3. ALWAYS TELL THE TRUTH (you'll get in less trouble)

# CHAPTER 3

# THIRD GRADE IS COMPETITIVE

My family has always been crazy competitive. Ever since I was little, everything we have done has become a game. Literally.

"Whose turn is it to clear the table?" Dad would ask.

"Rock. Paper. Scissors!" my brother and I would yell at the same time.

"Loser has to clean." I would always have to remind him.

Other times it would be a bigger deal. For example, family Scrabble night. Looking back, it could have been while we were playing Uno, a Play Station game, or even a game of HORSE outside on the basketball hoop. We always had to know what we were playing for before we started the game. Was it to see who had to clean the family room or make dinner? Would the loser have to vacuum or make popcorn for the family while we all watched TV that night? Sometimes the loser just had to do something embarrassing. Either way, there was always something to play for, so our competitive spirits grew.

My parents did try to teach us how to have good sportsmanship. If my brother and I were playing a game where someone lost and got upset, Mom was right there to make sure we didn't throw a fit. If we acted inappropriately, my mom would make us do something for not knowing how to lose graciously. If we won and gloated, she was there to teach us a lesson about that too. She wanted to make sure we knew that having good sportsmanship was not only about losing with dignity but also winning with class and respect.

By the time we started playing competitive sports, we already liked how it felt to win. I made it my mission to make it to the championship for Little League softball that year. The Bulldog Divas were going to go all the way, with my amazing bat, of course. We started winning and never looked back. Before we knew it, we were 10-0 and headed to the playoffs. It was a double-elimination tournament.

"I can't believe we get to lose in this tournament and still move on," I complained. "Losers shouldn't be allowed to move on after a loss."

"That is not very polite," Mom criticized. "Everyone has bad days. You never know what is going on with someone on any given day."

"Fine. Whatever." I laughed and smiled at my mom.

The first game of the tournament was a struggle. One girl couldn't be there, two girls were sick and not playing well, and me, well, we can just say that my bat was far from amazing. Truthfully, my bat was just plain awful. We lost that game 9-3. We were devastated.

The other team started screaming and chanting. "You guys suck!" "How were you all undefeated?" and "You're a team of losers – just go home now!"

I left the field feeling defeated. I remember thinking my mom was right: You never know what can happen.

Four games and four wins later, we were in the championship game, playing the number 2 seeded team. They were a great team. We had to be focused and bring our A-game. We worked as a team, and we worked hard. We won the championship game 8-5.

When it was over, I made sure we showed good sportsmanship. I did not want the other team to feel the way we did a few nights before. I turned around as our team was walking off the field and saw the other team was in tears. I ran to the opponent's dugout.

I walked up to their captain and held out my hand. "I just wanted to tell you I think your team was a great competitor. You all played so well."

"Thanks," she whispered. It was all she could get out.

"Good luck in your future tournaments," I said.

She smiled and thanked me. I ran back to my team. As I looked up, I saw my mom smile and touch her heart. I knew that I meant she was proud of me.

The funny thing was, I didn't expect it to feel so good. I guess that is part of why they call it 'good sportsmanship.' I knew then I would always have to remember that moment.

When I got home that night, I grabbed a Sharpie and opened my closet door. I added lesson number 4.

LESSONS LEARNED

1. NEVER PUT A SQUARE PEG IN A ROUND HOLE

2. ALWAYS BE KIND

3. ALWAYS TELL THE TRUTH (you'll get in less trouble)

4. DON'T FORGET TO HAVE GOOD SPORTSMANSHIP

The next day I added a picture of the trophy next to the fourth lesson. It would always help me remember how I felt.

# CHAPTER 4

# FOURTH GRADE AND FRIENDSHIP HARDSHIPS

Fourth grade: a.k.a. the year where you're almost the oldest kid in school. You better believe I was getting ready to run JB White Elementary. Then, BAM! I found out we were moving out of state. New school, new teachers, new friends... new problems.

Moving that year brought new friendships and some quite unpleasant relationships. I had to deal with cliques, stereotypes, and mean girls, and I was only 9 years old.

I remember coming home from school and telling my mom that a group of girls had been whispering, giggling, and pointing at me. They talked and stared at me. It made me feel awful all the time. It affected me in so many ways.

"You don't belong here," one would snicker.

"Why are you talking? No one was talking to you," snorted one of her followers.

"You're a nobody!"

At first, I would only cry at night when no one could see me. However, as time went on, they started saying things during every class, and the names got worse. I started to come home in tears. My mom helped me to see how their words were only words. They could not hurt me if I didn't let them.

My mom's advice was to look for the best in them and use those qualities to help me be nice. She told me that sometimes the best way to deal with mean girls is to actually be especially nice to them. I thought the idea was crazy and that my mom was crazier.

I was pretty sure these girls had a voodoo doll of me at one of their houses. I thought about her suggestion, though. I was able to find some things that the girls did that I complimented them on. One girl was good at art, one played basketball, and I think the third had a brother like me.

I wondered what would happen if I was nice to them instead of being intimidated. It took a lot of self-confidence to do what I did, but I had to try something, and I had to try it fast. I was getting clobbered in class.

Before class started the next day, I walked up to one of the girls. "That's a cool drawing. I like your use of colors."

"Thhhhaaaannnnkkk yoouuuu?" I heard her stutter back softly with an almost blank, slightly confused expression on her face.

At lunch, I went up to a different one of the girls and wished her good luck at her basketball game that night. She didn't say anything but looked up, smiled, and nodded.

The only one left was the one who did most of the whispering. I didn't know what to say to her. I just smiled as I walked by. If I couldn't find the best in her, I just hoped there was good in there. She didn't smile back that day, but after a few days of doing this, she did. The whispering slowly died down. As the weeks went by, I stopped feeling their stares on the back of my neck.

I couldn't believe my mom's plan had worked. Within a few weeks, I could confidently say they totally stopped talking bad about me and even started to be nice. They started short conversations with me. Sometimes they would even ask me questions. We didn't become best friends, and that was ok with me. I enjoyed knowing I changed the situation by seeing the best in others and making a change.

I felt so good about what I had accomplished that I decided I needed to help others. I was hoping my new knowledge could help others gain some courage for themselves.

First, I went and asked my teacher to teach a lesson on being kind. Some kids needed to be reminded of how to do this and how it can affect others.

Second, I figured if I needed help on how to deal with getting bullied every day, others might need help with that too. I kept my eyes open to see if there was ever an opportunity to help someone in need.

As the year continued, I knew I needed to add two things to my door. These were big lessons that I would always need to remember. As I stared at my closet with Sharpie in hand, I prayed that I would always be strong enough to remember these lessons and continue to help others learn from them as well.

LESSONS LEARNED

1. NEVER PUT A SQUARE PEG IN A ROUND HOLE

2. ALWAYS BE KIND

3. ALWAYS TELL THE TRUTH (you'll get in less trouble)

4. DON'T FORGET TO HAVE GOOD SPORTSMANSHIP

5. TRY TO SEE THE BEST IN OTHERS

6. BE KIND: NO BULLYING

# CHAPTER 5

# FIFTH GRADE AND FIGURING OUT WHO YOU ARE

Fifth grade sure was harder than I thought. The teachers kept saying things to scare us all year long. "Just wait 'til you get into middle school," was their favorite line of all. They started that one in the first week!

When you're in 5th grade, you are expected to become more mature and responsible at home too. I knew, though, I didn't feel that different. I knew I didn't want to clean my room more than before. I didn't want to be nicer to my brother either.

I did want to be treated like I was older, though. I guess that is why it was hard at home. I wanted to do one thing, and my parents wanted me to do another. Sometimes we agreed. Sometimes I felt like they were treating me like a baby. Sometimes I felt like they were making me do too much. I just wanted to play. Understanding family was hard.

Friendships were no walk in the park either.

Recess wasn't as much playing as it used to be; kids used it as a time to see who talked to whom.

There were popular and not popular groups.

Boys and girls started to like each other. Like more than friends!

Playdates had less actual playing in them too.

Cliques were tighter, and mean girls got meaner.

...

To make matters worse, in fifth grade, you try to find who you are.

Are you a leader or a follower?

Are you going to help someone when they need it or kick them when they are down?

Are you going to remain friends with someone no matter what group they end up in, or only if they are popular?

Will you talk about your friend behind their back if others are, or will you be the one to stand up for them?

Are you going to be the kind of friend people want to be friends with?

Overall, fifth grade taught me a lot of things, but mostly it came down to who I wanted to be and how was I going to get there.

When I got home from my last day of school, I took a Sharpie out of my pencil bag. Before I went outside to celebrate, I went to my closet. I knew what my number 7 was going to say.

LESSONS LEARNED

1. NEVER PUT A SQUARE PEG IN A ROUND HOLE

2. ALWAYS BE KIND

3. ALWAYS TELL THE TRUTH (you'll get in less trouble)

4. DON'T FORGET TO HAVE GOOD SPORTSMANSHIP

5. TRY TO SEE THE BEST IN OTHERS

6. BE KIND: NO BULLYING

7. SCHOOL IS HARD, FAMILY IS HARD, & SOMETIMES FRIENDSHIPS ARE THE HARDEST

# FIFTH GRADE

# PART 2 – SAVE THE DRAMA FOR ... ANYONE ELSE!

Summer always brought fun, memories, tans, and DRAMA. This summer was no exception.

I loved hanging out with my friends, going to the pool, and enjoying our time off. Everything was going great until I started talking to girls from a different group of friends. My best friends called them the 'other clique'. These girls weren't as funny. They didn't seem as nice either, but they were popular.

It all started when we were at the pool one hot summer day in June. I was sitting with Mae and Jordan, our feet dangling in the deep end. The sun glistened off the pool, and we were enjoying how the water cooled us off. We had music blaring the best summer songs. We had a cooler of popsicles and not a care in the world. We spent all day laughing and having people come up to us to talk or swim by and smile. We had girls chatting with us and hanging out. We had some boys come up to us to say hello, splash us, or just ask us for popsicles. Some even hung out a bit in our corner of the pool. It must have looked as fun as it was because the two most popular girls in our grade spent the day glaring at us from their lounge chairs. They didn't come over, but every time I looked their way, they were staring over their sunglasses or from behind their phones in our direction. They didn't talk to us, but I could swear they wanted to. Their phones were just a facade for what they were actually staring at all day.

The next day we went back and did the same thing. That afternoon, we seemed to get attention from a few more of the 'cool' boys. We all splashed each other as we floated on our rafts in the deep end. Some of the boys would jump off the diving board right where we were just to hit us with the splashes and make our rafts go crazy. Sometimes they got so close we could barely stay on them. We laughed all afternoon.

Eventually, the two girls who had been staring at us for two days now glided over to where we were all hanging out. Mae looked up and saw them sit on the edge of the pool; she just rolled her eyes. Jordan just ignored them and kept talking to whoever was listening to her. I got nervous. I don't know why, but I felt like something in the atmosphere had changed. I knew them even coming to be near us could end up being a big deal.

This one event, as silly as it sounded, could change our summer if we played our cards right. I loved my two best friends more than anything, but I wanted to be the other girls' friend too, to be known as popular. As they turned around to put their feet in the pool water, I turned and looked at them. I gave them a dazzling smile, and they returned it.

Charlotte spoke first. "It's LilyAnna, right?" she asked as she adjusted the towel she was sitting on.

Before I could be upset that she didn't know how to say my name, one of the boys we were swimming with quickly turned to her. "It's LilyAnn," Lucas corrected. I no longer cared that they didn't know how to say my name because Lucas was sweet enough to tell her. It made me blush. I looked at him and mouthed, 'Thank you.' Charlotte put her hand to her face, making sure it looked like she was incredibly embarrassed.

"I'm so sorry. That's what I meant." Charlotte gushed apologies in my direction. I made sure she knew I didn't care. I waved her apologies off. Jordan and Mae just rolled their eyes in her direction and then looked straight at me. Charlotte smiled slyly in the direction of the boys, ignoring the girls, and asked, "Do you mind if we join you? It looks like you all are having so much fun."

"Not at all!" I smiled. I couldn't believe they wanted to hang with us.

"Yes, we do!" Mae and Jordan both answered at the same time, and the boys turned and giggled. They were not used to anyone saying no to Charlotte. Charlotte and Raegan glared daggers in my friends' direction; they were not used to 'no' either. After the four of them had a stare-down, Charlotte and Raegan brought their gaze back to me. I smiled weakly at them. It was hard to focus on what I should say since I could still hear the boys giggling slightly under their breath, and I knew Mae and Jordan were still scowling hard at Charlotte and Raegan.

I whipped my head in their direction and gave my friends a pleading look. I knew there was desperation in my eyes. I could tell they didn't agree with how I felt, but they didn't say anything else. They huffed and turned back around to face the boys. They threw a beach ball in the air to start playing a game, just so they didn't have to respond to me. I immediately turned back to face Charlotte and Raegan.

They took my reaction as an invitation to join us. They chatted on and on about what they had done this summer and what they still wanted to do. I would like to say we all talked, but really, I mostly just listened to them talk and nodded my head in what I hoped were the right spots. I smiled at them and laughed when I thought they said something witty. There wasn't much I thought was witty, so sometimes I just laughed when they threw their heads back and laughed.

Overall, it wasn't a stimulating conversation, but it was a conversation nonetheless. It was a conversation with the two girls who could change the way middle school would go for me if I played their game correctly. That then made it one of the most important conversations I had ever had up to that point in my life. Dramatic as it may sound, that is just how much power I thought Charlotte could have on my time in middle school.

As our conversation came to an end, she smiled brightly at me. I felt luck going in my direction. It was then that Charlotte looked over to where the boys were in the pool.

"So, Lucas, are you, JR and everybody still coming over this weekend for my kick-off to summer BBQ?" Charlotte's gaze didn't leave his face while she waited for his answer. Lucas looked around, a bit uncomfortable. He made sure to make eye contact with some of the other boys to get their responses before he answered.

"Ummm, ya. We're all still planning on coming," he replied.

"Great!" Charlotte beamed. She then turned her focus to me and gave me a bright smile. "I'm assuming you'll come too now, LilyAnn. I'll text you my information. Let me have your number."

"That sounds like a lot of fun," I told her. I rattled off my phone number as she typed it into her phone. She continued to type for a minute, hit send, and then threw her phone on the towel.

"There, all done!" she exclaimed. "You now have my address and all the details about the party. I'll let you know what colors Raegan and I are wearing when we decide. You can coordinate your colors with ours. It'll be fabulous fun. Everyone who is anyone will be there."

"OK", I stammered. I had never expected there to be a dress code for what I was going to wear to a party. I also never thought they would want to include me in any of their plans; getting invited was a big enough honor. So, matching outfits it was! My head was dizzy with all the new events of the day. Then I realized Mae and Jordan did not get invited.

I turned around to face the group. I wasn't ready to face Mae and Jordan, so I focused on the boys first. Lucas smiled at me when I met his eyes. He told me he was happy I was going to the party before he and the boys waved and swam off. I thought my heart couldn't pound any more than it was, but I was wrong. I took a deep breath and started to slowly turn all the way around to face my largest mirrors, the faces of Mae and Jordan.

I met their eyes, and at first, there was only silence. All you could hear was the background noise of kids laughing and splashing, kids jumping in the water, and music. Then, it wasn't silent anymore.

"Are you kidding me?" Jordan snarled at me. She somehow sounded both mad and hurt at the same time. "I can't believe you said you'd go, especially when she didn't invite us. In front of us!"

"I'm sorry! I didn't know how to say no to that offer. And I agree, it was so rude of her to invite me and not you guys. But I know you wouldn't have gone if she did ask either of you. And the thing is, I want to go! What if I just go and check it out? I won't stay long, and I'll come right home after and tell you all about it!" I know my idea was average at best, but I was hoping to go and not feel so guilty about it.

My best friends, my friends since before we could walk, just stared at me. For the first time in our lives, they were at a loss for words with me. I could see it. "Whatever." Was all Mae muttered, and then they both turned around and started to get out of the pool. They grabbed their towels and put them on, all while their backs still faced me. I felt bad. I felt bad that I was invited, and they weren't. I felt bad that I said yes right in front of them, knowing they were not going to like it. I felt bad, but I was still excited inside. I took a second to pull myself together, and then I got out of the pool. We all packed up in silence. For the time being, we were at an understanding. They knew I would go; I knew they didn't like that I was going. It wasn't perfect, but it was understood for now, and boy was I excited about going.

...

That was the beginning of the end. There were a bunch of awkward moments after that day in the pool. It was unlike anything I had ever felt with my friends before. It led to the beginning of a summer division between us. I wanted to hang with Charlotte and her sidekick Raegan sometimes, while Mae and Jordan thought it was a ridiculous waste of time. They wanted no part of hanging with those girls, which was fine since Charlotte and Raegan didn't want to hang with them either. The only person going crazy was me.

I struggled with the idea of my two groups of friends not liking each other.

I struggled to figure out what I should and shouldn't do.

...

One night, towards the end of the summer, Mae and Jordan were both sleeping over at my house. We were watching a movie on Netflix when I started to get this funny feeling in my stomach.

"What if I go my whole life being ordinary, never making a difference? I mean, that would be okay and all, but I always thought I would do or be something special. I'm scared I'll be ordinary," I said.

They looked at each other and smiled. Mae spoke first. "You are a lot of things, LilyAnn. Ordinary is not one of them. No matter what happens, you will figure out how to do something spectacular with your life. You will make a difference. You were born to be a square peg among all the round holes in this town. In this world! You just have to remember that."

A single tear fell down my face, and I tackled her. That is exactly what I needed to hear. Only true friends could bring something up from the past at exactly the right moment. They remembered I loved the game with the wooden hammer and shaped pegs. They remember I never liked to follow the rules; I enjoyed being different and blazing my own path. Not every kid would make the square peg go in the circle hole. Not only did they remember, but they even loved me for it. I felt better. I was ready for whatever middle school brought.

I thought.

I decided to make number eight of my list of lessons learned a new and improved version of the first. I may have started my school years by listening to my teachers tell me what I could or could not do, but now I felt like I had to trust my gut. I had to stand out. I had to be a square peg amongst all the circles. I got out a Sharpie and wrote lesson eight.

LESSONS LEARNED

1. NEVER PUT A SQUARE PEG IN A ROUND HOLE

2. ALWAYS BE KIND

3. ALWAYS TELL THE TRUTH (you'll get in less trouble)

4. DON'T FORGET TO HAVE GOOD SPORTSMANSHIP

5. TRY TO SEE THE BEST IN OTHERS

6. BE KIND: NO BULLYING

7. SCHOOL IS HARD, FAMILY IS HARD, & SOMETIMES FRIENDSHIPS ARE THE HARDEST

8. ALWAYS REMEMBER TO BE A SQUARE PEG IN A WORLD OF ROUND HOLES

# CHAPTER 6

# FIRST DAY OF SIXTH GRADE

I woke up before my alarm went off. I jumped out of bed and ran to the window. It was a beautiful, sunny day, and I was radiating with excitement.

The first day of sixth grade was finally here! I was so ready to be in middle school. In middle school, you got to walk the halls without all the little kids everywhere. You got to change classes every period without the teacher leading you in the hallway. You got to pick what goes in your locker, and no adult would check. I was going to be so grown up.

I knew my first day wasn't going to go as smoothly as I wanted; I had never been that lucky. I needed a plan. I stepped away from the window and headed over to my desk. I grabbed a Post-It from behind all the nail polishes. Now, what to write with? What to write with? Somewhere behind all the picture frames and lip glosses, I saw a pink marker. I grabbed it and bit the top off with my teeth. I plopped down on my bed, belly first, knees bent, feet up. I thought about what I was going to write as my legs moved back and forth.

"OK. I need some goals. If I am going to be somebody at Rose Middle, I need a plan." I started jotting down a few bullet points.

### *Sixth Grade Goals*

- Be popular
- Have fun, but do good schoolwork
- Make it to seventh grade happy and alive

I knew the last goal sounded a bit silly, but I had been stuck in the middle of these friend triangles all summer. Mae and Jordan had expressed concerns all summer long about the other girls I had started to hang out with. Those conversations had never ended well, that's for sure.

"LilyAnn, you know you are a different person when you hang around Charlotte and Raegan. You act aloof. You're never really in our conversations when you are with us, you're always looking over your shoulder when we are out, and sometimes you don't call us back. Worst of all, you have forgotten plans we have made and ended up standing us up," Mae analyzed during our last sleepover of the summer this past week.

"Give me a break Mae," my eyes begged her. I knew it was a poor response. So, I tried to change the subject with a sweet smile.

"Don't do that, LilyAnn," Jordan begged, "Unfortunately, Mae is being pretty accurate right now." I knew it, I just didn't know what to do about it.

I just had to figure out how to either get them to give Charlotte and Raegan a chance or start to balance my time with both groups better. I had been friends with Mae and Jordan since I was a toddler. We had always been like sisters. Charlotte and Raegan were the cool kids, and they were talking to me! I couldn't pass up this opportunity.

Not when I was so close to having it all, popularity, and my best friends. Not with middle school starting.

Charlotte and Raegan made me just as crazy. When they complained, they didn't focus on how I was treating them though; they focused on putting down Mae and Jordan. They said things like, "Mae and Jordan will hold you back in middle school. They are so not popular. They are boring, and you are the only friend they have that anyone likes." I tried to stick up for my friends, I mean, I did, but I always felt like I was walking a thin line between the two groups and didn't always know what to say. When I stuck up for Mae and Jordan, they jumped on me for picking Mae and Jordan over them, so I stopped and didn't say anything else. I knew in my heart I was not being a good friend, but I stayed quiet. Right now, I had to focus on my reputation.

…

Ok! I needed to stop thinking about this summer. It was time to focus. I had to get moving, or I would be late on the first day of school. I jumped off the bed and stuck the Post-It with the goals I had just written on the back of my closet door with all of my life lessons. I was not sure why yet, but my gut knew they probably connected somehow. I grabbed the third outfit I had picked out so far that morning, hoping that it would be the last outfit I tried on that day.

Middle school was indeed harder. Getting dressed for middle school was harder already! I finished my hair and headed out the door with my goals fresh in my mind. As I walked to the bus stop, I tried to prepare for my first day of middle school. I prepared myself for the drama I was sure would come today. But it was middle school, and I was older. I thought surely I could handle whatever came my way.

...

Mae, Jordan, and I had been riding the same bus together since we started Kindergarten. We loved to use that time to catch up, talk, listen to music together or, talk with other friends of ours. Sometimes we used it to unwind from the morning craziness that was our home routine: Running around, getting ready, trying to grab a healthy breakfast while still making it to the bus stop on time. Our parents teased us that we should not have had that much to catch up on since we were either together or on the phone all the time, but we always did. We reminded them that a lot could happen from the time we got off our phones at night to the next morning. You just never knew. Whether we had something to catch up on or not doesn't matter. It was a tradition that we loved and that we never missed.

When I got to the bus stop, neither of them was there yet. I pulled out my phone to text them as a white SUV pulled up to the curb in front of me. Charlotte stuck her head out of the window.

"LilyAnn! Can you believe today has finally arrived? Get in the truck! I'll have my mom take you to school with us. We can talk about your outfit on the way. If you're going to be hanging with us this year, we are going to have to talk about what colors you cannot wear together."

I looked down at what I thought was the winning outfit of the day and frowned. What could be wrong with my sweater and jeans? I looked up and she was smiling at me.

"Come on!" she cheered.

"I don't know; I'm waiting for Mae and Jordan." I nervously sighed. I was not prepared for the drama to start before I even got on the bus! Of course, I wanted to go with Charlotte to school. It would be great to start my day that way. However, I loved the tradition with Mae and Jordan, and I couldn't imagine not getting on the bus with them. I was about to tell her that when she faked a slight cough to move me along. Our eyes connected and I didn't say anything.

"Ummm, hello. What is taking you so long to get into the car?" Charlotte hissed.

"I appreciate it, but I always take the bus with Mae and Jordan," I started to explain.

"Blah, blah, Mae, blah, blah, Jordan. Ugh!"

"Charlotte, please be nice," I begged.

"I'll stop if you get in this vehicle right now!"

I rolled my eyes and laughed a little. She smiled. I huffed. She clapped her hands. It was over. I knew it was. When I made up my mind to go with her I started to get excited. The only problem was my heart broke at the same time.

As I started to take a step into the street to get into Charlotte's car, it all started happening at once! I heard the bus pulling up to the bus stop behind us. Immediately I became aware of the bus, and I saw Mae and Jordan out of the corner of my eye. They were running as their backpacks bounced up and down, waving their hands feverishly to make sure I saw them. It broke my heart not to acknowledge them. Decisions, decisions, I had to think fast. I put my head down and pretended not to notice them. They continued to yell my name over and over as they waved their arms. My stomach was in knots because I wasn't moving toward them.

The bus was right behind us; I could smell the fumes. Their voices were getting louder; they were only a couple of houses away from me now. However, I decided without even thinking about it. My feet just started moving. I closed my eyes and continued walking right up to Charlotte's car. I opened the door and put my bag in the backseat. Then, I slid in and slammed the door shut.

"LilyAnn, wait up! We are here!" Jordan was yelling my name with such force I couldn't tell if her voice was cracking because she was tearing up or because she was so mad.

I heard Mae add, "Really?!" as I rolled up my window and we drove away. It was crazy. I wasn't sure when I decided to go with Charlotte, but I was in the car now. I had a pit feeling in my stomach letting me know my conscience didn't think I made the right decision. Well, what's done was done. At least I would be showing up to my first day at Rose Middle with the most popular girl in school instead of on an old, stinky, yellow school bus. I already liked my odds for the first day better. Now, if I could have only gotten that feeling of guilt to go away.

# CHAPTER 7

# RED CARPET TREATMENT

We turned into the school parking lot, and there were kids everywhere outside. Kids were in their cliques, laughing, talking, and hugging friends as they walked up. Some boys were playing basketball, and some were sitting on the stairs to the school. The knot in my stomach doubled in size as we got close to the drop-off point. My hands were starting to get sweaty from nerves, and my heart started to pound so fast that I swore Charlotte was going to be able to hear it. I wiped my hands on my jeans and took some deep breaths. The car stopped, I closed my eyes and took one more final breath, and then I opened the door to hop out of the backseat. I prayed I was ready. Ready for today and ready for the consequences of not getting on the school bus.

Everything started to look like it was in slow motion, like when you are watching a movie, and they emphasize an important part by going so slow. I saw kids start to look at us as we slammed the car doors shut. I saw arms shooting up to wave in our direction. I saw some of the boys' heads facing us. I mean, a lot of heads. I thought I must have been dreaming. It started just as I hoped it would. Just as I had always wanted middle school to start. Before I had another minute to appreciate what was going on around me, Raegan ran up to us, screeching her hellos. She was beaming at us as she threw her arms around our shoulders to give us hugs.

"I thought you two would never get here!" Raegan exclaimed. "Instead of looking for each of you, I get you both at once! Can you believe today is finally here?" Charlotte smiled and then told her to relax a little. Being too excited to be here did not make the best first impression, she told Raegan. Raegan immediately agreed and apologized. They both plastered on their well-practiced, polished, huge smiles.

Charlotte looked at each of us and said, "Let's start to mingle."

Raegan nodded and then flipped her wavy brown hair back and turned towards the school. When she flipped her hair like that, it made me laugh inside. It was code for either 'Let's get down to business' or 'Look at me'. Today, I felt it meant both. I nodded as well and turned towards the school entrance. Well, it was now or never, I thought, as I took my first steps toward this new adventure with my arms linked to theirs.

As we walked up the main path to the school, I contemplated her words. I never looked at going to school as mingling, but I understood exactly what she meant and saw the truth to it. I guess it had never occurred to me since I never walked into school feeling as popular as I did today. Yup, I knew I could get used to that feeling. That fact made the butterflies in my stomach from not riding the bus go away. It didn't make my heart slow down, though, because Charlotte, Raegan, and I were walking into Rose Middle School arm in arm. The happiness on my face was undeniable.

As we walked in the doors and turned the corner, kids were coming up to us from out of nowhere to ask Charlotte and Raegan about their summers. Everyone seemed to want to be near them. There were hugs and kisses, squeals, and high-fives. Girls were trying to get so close to them that some pushed others out of their way. I got blond curls whipped in my face as a girl I didn't know sprang into Charlotte's arms. She barely looked at me as she squeezed Charlotte. I could tell by Charlotte's expression she thought the hug was too tight or too overwhelming even for her, so I grabbed Charlotte's arm and slowly tore her away from the blond girl. The blonde girl didn't skip a beat. She just waved her goodbyes and bounced down the hallway.

I could tell some people were a little shocked to see us all together and some even looked amused. People smiled at me because I was with them. I was sure they wouldn't have noticed me otherwise. Either way, they were paying attention to me that day. I got a lot of:

"Oh, Hi, LilyAnn."

"Hope you had a great summer LilyAnn."

"So, you saw a lot of Charlotte and Raegan, huh? Bet your summer was fun."

I talked to more people in the first 5 minutes than I probably would have all day if I had taken the bus. The conversations with people were quick and not the most stimulating, but they were plentiful. That was a great start.

We turned the corner and walked down the hall to where my locker was located. Charlotte waited for me as I opened my locker and swung the door open. I stood there staring into my locker. What happened? There was pink contact paper everywhere, there was a mirror on the backside of the door, my name in glitter, and most impressively, a mini chandelier hung from the top and lit up when I opened my locker. I stood there with my mouth open. I turned and faced Charlotte and Raegan, who were all smiles. "You did this?" I asked them, truly full of shock.

Raegan nodded and said, "Now your locker will match ours. We came yesterday to do ours and wanted to surprise you. Your mom gave us your locker information when we told her we were surprising you."

"Thank you," is all I could get out. They each hugged me. I turned around and put what I needed into my locker and investigated my reflection in the mirror. I was truly beaming with delight.

As Charlotte rambled on about what class she had first and where she wanted to sit for lunch, my mind was racing to keep up with her. Just as I was about to tell her to take a breath, a couple of boys started walking straight for us. My hands started to sweat a bit again. I felt my legs get a little shaky. I concentrated to keep myself together, looked steady on my feet, and tried to relax, all at the same time. Phew. Groups of kids, especially boys, coming up to my locker before school even started had not been a regular thing for me in the past. What was I supposed to do? What was I supposed to say? I couldn't decide. I turned back around and put my head in my locker to grab my lip gloss and apply it in my new mirror. I stared at myself for a second. I couldn't believe my first thought was to put on makeup when I saw the boys. Who was I becoming?

In fifth grade, many boys had been my friends. We hung out all the time. They picked me up when we played tag at recess. I never got nervous being around any of them, even the most popular ones. How did one summer change the way I felt? I had so many thoughts going all over the place in my head. I had to remember to take a breath. I breathed in and turned around just as the boys were in front of us.

"Hey, Charlotte. Hi, LilyAnn," said JR. "How's it going?"

"What's up, girls?" Lucas smiled and I couldn't help but smile right back at him. He was always so friendly.

Charlotte immediately started to go on and on about the beach and the shopping she did the last few days before school started. She wanted all their attention as she gave them an abundant number of details and smiles. I understood her wanting their attention, but she was starting to bore even me. The boys were being polite and seemed to be listening. I couldn't get over it. I was barely listening. JR might have been the sweetest boy in the sixth grade and Lucas was adorable, but I was shocked they were paying attention to her.

I started to think about what I would have said if I had answered them first. I was not sure, but I did know that I was never going to turn into some crazy, over-talkative girl. I refused to go on and on like she was doing. As Charlotte continued talking, I thought to myself that they will appreciate me for that one day. I giggled quietly. .

Lucas turned his attention to me. I saw him looking at me from the corner of my eye, so I decided to turn, face him, and smile.

"How are you? How did your summer end?" Lucas asked me. I took a step closer to him since I could barely hear him over Charlotte talking about herself.

"I'm doing great. I ended my summer hanging out with friends and dancing a lot. How about you?" I asked as I beamed up at him.

"You sure sound like you were busy. I understand that. I played baseball almost all summer," Lucas replied. He put his head down for a second and said, "We should have tried to hang more."

"That would have been fun. I would have liked that." As I said it, I realized how much I meant it too. Lucas and I always had fun when we hung out.

We grinned at each other and slowly turned our attention back to Charlotte, just as her voice jumped up five octaves. We both let out a little giggle but kept our attention on Charlotte. I was so glad, too. If he had continued to look at me, he might have seen the blush that started to rise in my cheeks.

We were all at my locker. It was loud. It was crowded. It probably looked like fun because it was fun. I was laughing with Charlotte, Raegan, JR, and Lucas, along with whoever else stopped to join us. I loved the smiles and fun that surrounded me.

And then, just like that, I wasn't having fun anymore.

# CHAPTER 8

# REALITY CHECK

As I was laughing at something someone said, I didn't even know who or what it was for sure. I made eye contact. Just over Raegan's shoulder, I saw them. I was looking right at Mae and Jordan in the hallway. They were only a few feet away, yet it felt like we were standing on totally different planets. The knots that were in my stomach all came rushing back.

The bell rang, and everyone started to scatter to their first class. Wow. I would never be able to say I had a boring first day of middle school, and it was only 8:00 a.m.! However, I did have some damage control to do, and that did not feel good. I had to make things right with Mae and Jordan. But how? I decided I would make it right at lunchtime.

...

The middle school cafeteria. Period. It has been said it can make or break people on the first day of school. On any day of school, really. As soon as you open those glass doors, you have decisions to make, and you must make them fast! You only get one shot to make the right choice to set up your whole year. If it's a wrong choice, you could be sitting at the back table with the kids who don't talk to anyone and only eat the day-old mac and cheese. That couldn't be me. I needed to make good choices.

I took a deep breath and pushed the doors open. I looked to my right. Charlotte and Raegan were sitting with two other girls and a few boys at a long table near the windows. I looked to my left. Mae and Jordan were sitting at the end of a table that they were sharing with some girls who we had started talking to last year. When it came down to it, it wasn't a hard decision.

Deep breath number two. Time to make things right. I got lunch; turkey, mashed potatoes, and green beans, as well as something to drink. I turned around and walked past several tables, heading over to where Mae and Jordan were sitting. I pulled out a chair next to Mae and sat down. They both pretended not to see me. I looked like I was watching a tennis match, looking back and forth between the two of them. I gave them a few seconds, sitting in silence. Then I gave them both the best puppy dog eyes I could make. They still didn't respond. I laid my arm around Mae and positioned my face right up to Jordan. My eyes were as big as saucers, and I was whimpering. This got a smile out of Mae, but I knew I was not off the hook.

"What was that all about?" Jordan demanded. She seemed more upset.

"I'm sorry I didn't ride the bus with you today. That was unthoughtful."

"It was not okay. It is still not okay," Mae added. "It's not like riding the bus together is a new thing we were going to try to do for the first time this school year. To make matters worse, you still left even though we were yelling at you. Running and yelling at you. I don't understand how you could just get in the car and leave us on the street."

"Really, LilyAnn, we yelled for you for over a block. I was almost positive you heard us or at least saw us. Are you going to tell me you didn't?" Jordan pressed me.

I allowed myself exactly 3 seconds to come up with what to say. I could tell the truth and risk hurting my two oldest, best friends or I could lie. Really, I had no choice; I knew what I needed to do. I truly worried I would hurt them if I told the truth. I felt like such a brat for pretending not to see them. I would lie for them, and selfishly, for me.

"I am so sorry, you guys. I promise I didn't see or hear you. I thought maybe I missed the bus. Charlotte's mom came and asked if I wanted a ride, so I figured, why not? I didn't want to walk to school." I waited nervously as they considered my answer.

They both just stared at me and then at each other. This was new territory for all of us. We had never really fought. Nothing big anyway, like this morning. Jordan rolled her eyes at me. They each let out a sigh.

"Fine. Whatever," Mae finally spit out as she looked at me wearily. She was saying it was okay like we were good and it was over. Deep down, however, I knew it wasn't. I would have some more making up to do.

Just as I started to feel better about spending time with Mae and Jordan during lunch, I looked over at the long table by the windows. Charlotte made eye contact with me. She looked down at the empty seat next to her and then back to me and rolled her eyes. People really needed to stop doing that! I guess making everyone happy in the lunchroom was not going to happen. All I could do was hope for a better experience tomorrow.

# CHAPTER 9

# THERE'S ALWAYS A NEW KID

After lunch, I had English with Charlotte and Mae. Oh, good. That would be a lot of fun. Thank goodness Mrs. Eachus didn't let us pick where we wanted to sit. She had an actual stop sign as we walked in to make sure we didn't sit down until she had given us our assigned seat. I ended up sitting only one seat away from Charlotte and across the room from Mae. I felt a bit guilty that I was excited about this opportunity to be near my popular friend without having to choose and hurt my other friend. Thank you, Mrs. Eachus.

Each student gave her their name, and she then pointed in the direction of where their desk was located. As the last person was walking to the desk she was assigned, Mrs. Eachus started to introduce herself to the class. She paused when the classroom door slowly started to open. Like out of a movie, everyone turned and stared at the door. In walked a girl that I was sure no one recognized. She handed Mrs. Eachus a piece of paper; it looked like her schedule. Mrs. Eachus examined it, confirming she was in the right room. As she was looking at the paper, I stared at her. She looked nervous; I would have been too. Poor thing couldn't have even started her first day of middle school at the beginning of the day. She had to make an entrance to a class after lunch. She was standing there, alone, in front of the room. I watched her as she fidgeted with a string that was unraveling a little from her shirt. It seemed to have a small rip at the bottom. I immediately felt sorry for her. Mrs. Eachus assigned her to an empty desk. While she was walking slowly to her desk, I looked around the room. Everyone's eyes were on the new girl.

Well, she sure made an entrance. The only problem for her was that it wasn't a positive one. I turned in my chair and faced forward. I heard Charlotte already whispering about her to the group.

"Nice first day of school outfit. Where did she go shopping over the summer, Dumpsters R Us? I mean, was it the only thing that would fit her or the only thing that she could afford?" she laughed loudly.

Everyone else around her joined in and started laughing as well. I didn't laugh. I couldn't bring myself to, but I did the uncomfortable chuckle. The chuckle that says I heard you and acknowledge you said something, but I don't 100% agree with you. At least, that was what I was hoping the chuckle meant. Since we were talking about Charlotte here, I assumed she took my chuckle as, 'I agree with you, and you are super funny.' Oh, boy.

English class was kind of a blur after that. People sat quietly, people whispered, and students did the work that they were supposed to. I struggled with concentrating all period. I noticed Mae on the other side of the room with her head down, working hard on a task and sometimes talking to the person next to her. I noticed some kids around the new girl who turned their backs toward her while they were still sitting in their desk chairs. I heard Charlotte talking to the people around us as she threw back her head and smiled. I saw Mrs. Eachus helping students, staying by the new girl's desk a little bit longer than anyone else's.

I watched everyone in the room. I had that feeling in my stomach where I knew something had just happened that was about to change the course of my life. Like, you're just sitting there, yet your heart beats a little faster, you can't concentrate on anything, your stomach's butterflies start to dance just a little, and you don't know why exactly. Maybe it was the devilish look in Charlotte's eyes or the pleading look in Mae's that I noticed. Maybe it was the way the new girl kept playing with the unraveling thread of her shirt. Or maybe it was just 6$^{th}$ grade English class, and I was not doing as good of a job balancing all the drama as I thought I would have been. I couldn't say. I just accepted the blur and prayed for the best for the rest of the day.

...

My last period of the day was PE. Seriously, it's bad enough that every middle schooler is required to take PE, but to give it to a whole class of 6$^{th}$ graders at the end of the day, seemed like both a funny joke and a punishment. Someone must have been out of their minds when they scheduled PE last period for any student. When I calmed down and remembered that I can't change the situation right now or for the rest of the year, I tried to find the positives to having PE last period instead. I may not like the idea of having to change out of my very cute, calculated outfit at the end of each day, but I was looking forward to blowing off a ton of steam at the end of each day. I felt like I was going to need that opportunity on more than one occasion this year. Since we lost recess in middle school and the drama was amped up about 1000%, blowing off steam did sound like a great way to end the day. Steam from sitting quietly all day long in class. Steam from the stress of the lunchroom. Steam from friend triangles. Basically, steam from being in middle school.

I walked into the PE locker room, ready to get the period started and over with. Come on. Positive thoughts. I was a little relieved that I didn't have Charlotte, Raegan, Mae, or Jordan in my PE class. It would be easier to focus on feeling better at the end of the day. I wouldn't always be thinking about what one of them was thinking or doing, knowing they would be watching me. So, I didn't have PE with any girls I was friends with, but as luck would have it, I did have it with the new girl. I heard the teacher talking to her. Her name was Jessica. I tried not to stare while they were talking, but I found myself curious about her.

She found a locker near the back of the locker room and didn't talk to anyone as she opened it. The few people that did walk by her didn't say anything to her. She kept her head down, staring at the floor. Just when I had decided to stop looking at her, she walked past where I was changing. I was not sure where she was going since she was still in the clothes she had worn to school. I continued to watch her to see where she ended up. She very discreetly walked into the teacher's office and came back out with rental clothes. She put them behind her back and walked quickly to her locker. I was full of questions. Did she forget her PE uniform at home? Did she forget to buy one at registration? I watched her as she shoved them into her locker. I didn't know her, but I sure hoped they washed those rentals over the summer, for her sake!

All dressed and ready to go, I walked into the gym. As we started to line up on the gym floor for attendance, I noticed Lucas was also in my PE class. I let out a breath I didn't even know I was holding. I did have a friend in my class. PE was going to be just fine. Maybe even better than fine.

As we were being put in our spots for attendance and stretches, I looked for Lucas. He ended up five rows away from me. It was too hard to try to get his attention now. I started to look around to see who was by me. I found myself near Jessica. I didn't see anyone else that I knew. Again, I had another decision to make. I felt like I had been making hard decisions all day that focused on my social life and what was right and wrong. It had been a very mentally exhausting day. So, I thought to myself, I could stand all by myself while Lucas talked to a group of boys, or I could start a conversation with Jessica. Which would make me look worse? Oh, my goodness! I couldn't believe I was having this conversation with myself. Who cared what others thought? Decision made. Of course, being nice and talking to a new student was the best thing to do.

"Hi. I'm LilyAnn. You're Jessica, right? I'm in your English class." I introduced myself and smiled.

"Hi," Jessica whispered.

"So, how do you like our school so far? Is it different from where you came from?

"It's okay, I guess. It's a lot bigger, and there are a lot more kids."

I thought for a second about how I would handle a change like that going into middle school. "I bet that must be hard to get used to. I hope it gets easier for you." I meant what I said. It made Jessica smile at me.

Before we could say anything else, the whistle blew to start class. As the teacher went through the roll call, I thought about English class and our conversation just now. Why was that pit in my stomach coming back? Jessica seemed nice. Shy, but nice. I was sure she would be able to make friends soon. Right? Hmmm. The pit in my stomach was reminding me that might not have been the case.

After PE, we all headed back to the locker room. I started to change into the outfit that had taken me forever to pick out that morning. The one that I was not sure Charlotte approved of me wearing. Amazingly, even though I had just had PE, I felt like I still looked cute. It was a nice way to end a crazy day. Now, all I had to do before the day was over was remember to catch the bus home with Mae and Jordan, or they wouldn't talk to me until high school.

# CHAPTER 10

# HAS IT ONLY BEEN A WEEK?

The first week of middle school.

My first week of middle school.

Is it always this stressful for everyone?

I swore this had been the hardest week of my life. I was exhausted. Besides trying to figure out the academic part of all my classes, I felt like I was trying to be two different people. I was so torn all the time. I was trying to make sure I hung with Mae and Jordan as much as we always had before, but it was getting harder and harder to fit them into my schedule with all the social demands Charlotte and Raegan had put on me.

Besides all the things they wanted to do after school – shopping, trying on matching outfits, or just walking around together – they were starting to make it hard for me to talk to Mae and Jordan during the day as well. Every time I tried to leave their sides to find Mae or Jordan, they acted like I was breaking all kinds of social rules.

"LilyAnn!" Mae yelled down the hallway after first period. I stopped and smiled. As I turned to start walking toward her, Charlotte put her arm through my arm and turned me back around. As she was chatting away, she put a tighter squeeze on my arm and started trying to walk away. I immediately put on my breaks and got her to stop moving. I let out a small, silent breath and turned to face her.

"I'll just be a minute." I smiled up at Charlotte and wiggled out of her grasp. "I promise. I will be right back." Charlotte made a production about it, but she let go of my arm.

I quickly jogged back down the hallway to where I had last seen Mae.

"Hey, Mae. Hey, Jordan. How are you guys? Sorry I missed you this morning before the first bell. I didn't see you guys in the hallway at all." I tried to sound like I had looked all over for them.

The truth was that Charlotte and Raegan wouldn't let me leave their lockers. It was a ritual now to stand there so everyone knew where to find us in the morning. Tons of people in 6th (and even 7th!) grade spent all morning coming up to talk to us. It was crazy.

They both rolled their eyes a little. "I'm sure it is hard to look for us when you are at your locker station," Jordan replied. Mae chuckled under her breath. "I'm just guessing." I had no response. I was busted.

"I was looking for you, though. Anyway, you know you guys can always come up and talk to me when you see me there. It would be fine." I tried to reason with them.

"Maybe fine for you, but we know they won't be fine with that," Jordan replied, her voice sounding sour.

"Besides," Mae started in right after, "We want to talk to you, not listen to Charlotte and Raegan go on and on. And they do go on and on and on and on."

"I get that, I guess." I conceded. We all stood there silently for a minute, knowing we still hadn't accomplished anything but not knowing what else to say.

"I love ya both," was all I came up with. I gave them my famous puppy dog eyes. Those had always gotten them both to laugh. As Mae was saying something about how I am lucky they know I love them, Charlotte came up behind me and put her arm through my arm again. I immediately started to jerk my arm, but before I could move, Raegan grabbed my other arm. I swore they were holding on so tight that I felt like an actual prisoner in handcuffs. I could only imagine what this looked like to Mae and Jordan.

"Sorry to interrupt, girls," Raegan barked, however, we really must go. We need LilyAnn." They both pulled me away before I could say a single word. Even though they dragged me away as fast as they could, it didn't stop me from hearing the things Mae and Jordan were saying to each other. I was going to hear about this at lunch, and I knew I deserved it.

...

I sat in all my morning classes worried about lunch, worried about what Mae and Jordan were going to say to me. I was not sure if I was more upset about what they were going to say or if it was because I knew I deserved it. No one should leave in the middle of talking to their best friends the way I did. I sure hoped they had some comfort food in the cafeteria for lunch. I needed some French fries.

...

RING RING RING

The lunch bell rang, so I set off for lunch. This used to be the most fun part of the day, but now I just get stressed out every time I open the large glass doors to the cafeteria. I got my lunch, which did not consist of any French fries today, and sat beside Mae. We were still in the small talk stage, not talking about what we all knew we needed to discuss.

This was honestly okay with me since I missed the simple, small talk we all always shared. As I began to eat my salad, I saw Jordan shift her eyes and put her head down to look at her sandwich. I got a pit in my stomach; I knew drama was coming. I finished the bite of salad in my mouth and looked back down the aisle between all the lunchroom tables. Charlotte was strolling up the aisle, heading to our table with Raegan close on her heels. I didn't even get a second bite of my salad down before it all began.

"LilyAnn dear," Charlotte purred loudly, "you really must eat with us today so we can discuss the small party I'll be hosting at my house. It's quite important, so you must help me out." She waited with her hands on the table, not moving. I felt like I was on a reality TV show, with everyone waiting to see what I would do next. Mae and Jordan looked from Charlotte to Raegan and then back to me. Charlotte and Raegan looked from me to Mae and Jordan and then back to me. It was impossible to describe how I was feeling at that moment. Suddenly, all four of them were staring at me, just waiting for me to respond.

Raegan was more impatient with the game of who would speak first than the rest of them. She huffed and stomped her foot like a child, "What is taking you so long to get up? Let's go!"

She sounded like a brat. I didn't say it though.

I took a deep breath and slowly let it out. I looked up at Charlotte and Raegan. "Fine. I'll be right there. Just go sit back down at your table." With smug smiles on their faces, they skipped off down the aisle. I found myself staring at them as they left. Not because they were doing anything interesting, but because I was too scared to turn around and face my best friends. After a few seconds, I finally turned to look at them.

Jordan broke the silence before I could try to explain. "Are you serious? You are getting up and leaving us in the middle of lunch? To party plan for Charlotte? After this morning. I am done, LilyAnn. I can't keep feeling like we are second to them. Them, of all people! It hurts too much."

"Me too this time." Mae agreed. "If you walk away, don't bother talking to us for a while. We will need to take a break from this drama."

I looked at each of them, one at a time. I began to feel sick to my stomach. I knew why. I knew it was because I was making the wrong decision again, but I was going to make it anyway. I made it without really thinking at all. As I slowly got up from the table, I looked at them and gave them a weak smile. With pain in my heart, I started to walk away. As I did, I whispered, "I hope you don't mean that." And then I left.

...

The bell finally rang. Lunch was over. Thank goodness. It was hard to not look over at Mae and Jordan while I listened to Charlotte go on and on about trivial details for her party. As the bell rang, I felt a quick moment of relief that lunch was over. The relief was short-lived, though. English class was next. English meant I got to sit by Charlotte and feel Mae's laser eyes burning a hole into my head. No, make that my soul. Why was trying to be popular so hard? Was it wrong that I liked that Charlette and Raegan had added me to their clique? Was it bad that I liked that Lucas was talking to me more that year than he ever had? I knew the answer. It wasn't necessarily bad, but it wasn't necessarily good either.

I walked into class and laid my school bag on the floor next to my desk. As I slipped into the desk, I heard Charlotte already at it. She was making all the kids around us crack up while Mrs. Eachus started to take attendance. I turned all the way around in my chair, so I could hear better. She wasn't saying anything particularly witty or even funny for that matter. She was just being mean. She was making fun of the new girl, Jessica. Again. She was pointing out that she had worn almost the same outfit for most of the week. She added the idea that it might be because they didn't sell clothes her size at Goodwill.

This didn't feel right. No one should be made fun of for what they can afford, especially not for their size. I realized Charlotte was being sneaky. She wasn't saying all these mean things to Jessica's face, but anyone could tell by the way Jessica was shuffling in her chair she could hear the whole conversation. I assumed that was Charlotte's plan. That was just as bad. I could tell that Mae could hear Charlotte too.

Mae and I made eye contact, and she just shook her head at me. I knew what Mae was thinking. She was thinking the same thing I was about this situation. The whole thing was horrible. My big worry was that she would think I was okay with it all since Charlotte was the one being mean. I wasn't, but what was I supposed to do about it? It *was* Charlotte after all.

As Charlotte was about to describe what she thought about Jessica's hair in full detail, Mrs. Eachus began class. Phew. At least she was done with her for now. However, something in my gut told me Charlotte was just getting started on poor, innocent Jessica.

...

Boy was I right. Charlotte continued to talk about Jessica, even when she was not around, including when we sat in Charlotte's room watching T.V. after school that day. Her room was just how someone might imagine it to be. There was a large, four-post bed in the center, with comfy chairs spread out around her television. She had a bright pink comforter and pink walls that were full of posters, pictures, and mirrors.

I was draped over one of her chairs with my head hanging over the edge. I lay there staring at the ceiling. I thought I was coming over to watch the latest movie on Netflix that we had planned to watch together, but instead, she was still acting like a stand-up comedian who had gleefully found their next focus for all their jokes. The focus? Jessica of course. Raegan was watching T.V. more than she was listening to Charlotte go on and on and crack herself up. Now and then, Raegan laughed to make Charlotte feel like she had her attention, but I could tell she didn't. She had mine, though. I was getting frustrated. I had finally had enough.

"Charlotte, please let it go. You don't have to like her, but you don't have to keep talking about her either. It's exhausting." I pleaded.

Raegan whipped around from the T.V. as soon as I asked Charlotte to let it go. Her mouth hung open as she stared at me in disbelief. I was pretty much one hundred percent sure she had never talked to Charlotte that way. She kept looking from me to Charlotte, from me to Charlotte.

"Excuse me, LilyAnn. You want me to stop talking?" Charlotte hissed, her face getting redder as the seconds ticked by.

"It's not that I want you to stop talking. I just want to talk about something besides Jessica," I reassured her. Her face scrunched up. I could tell she did not like that I was questioning what she was doing. I tried to think of something else to say so that her head wouldn't explode.

"Besides, I would much rather hear you talk about the outfits we are going to wear tomorrow. You always have such great ideas for us," I gushed and shot her a dazzling smile. I was just hoping my redirection of topics, along with the compliment, would get us off the Jessica topic without her getting mad at me.

It was silent for a few seconds. Raegan stared from me to Charlotte, not saying a word. I swore I could hear the ticking of the seconds passing on my watch. It was so quiet. Finally, she broke the silence.

"You're right. I would much rather talk about what we are going to wear instead of what she's wearing." Charlotte announced. I couldn't believe it worked without her getting upset. Raegan relaxed and turned back towards the T.V. Charlotte started talking about what we should wear to school tomorrow. I just smiled at her while she talked, grateful the Jessica conversation was over.

# CHAPTER 11

# CHARLOTTE'S PARTY

Today was the day: Charlotte's party. The party I had helped her plan down to the last detail. The party that was the breaking point for Mae and Jordan that day I had left them sitting at our lunch table. It still made me sad when I thought about how I had chosen this party idea over Mae and Jordan. I often had regrets.

I decided to put the thoughts of Mae and Jordan out of my head for the day. What was done was done, and I was due over at Charlotte's house soon so we could all get ready together. I had a feeling getting ready for this party was going to be a production. I packed all the things Charlotte and Raegan told me to pack, as well as a few extra things I might need just in case.

I headed over to her house with a storm of things going on in my head. Should I stop by and see the girls on my way? No. That was a horrible idea. I would feel so bad they weren't invited that I would never leave their houses. Should I ask my mom to come and pick me up right where I was walking and have her take me to dinner and a movie to avoid any potential drama? No. That would be social suicide. Do I put my air pods in, pick a song, and relax as I head over? Yes. That is what I will do to help me relax and get ready for my first official middle school party.

Boy, was I right. Getting ready was a production like I had never been a part of before. It took us over an hour to get dressed and do our hair. Charlotte wanted the three of us to look perfect. Does anyone ever *really* look perfect? I would have been happy just wearing jeans and a sweater to a party with friends, but that was not the vision Charlotte had for us, so I was wearing a dress. We were all wearing dresses in the same color. Charlotte felt that this would help us stand out in a crowd. She always wanted to stand out in any crowd. I wondered if she told people not to wear purple since that is what we were all wearing. Honestly, I wouldn't doubt it.

...

The first guests started to arrive promptly at 7:00 pm. The number of students that were here was impressive. I was most impressed that some $7^{th}$ and $8^{th}$ graders showed up as well. I had never been to a party with so many older kids before. I moved around the room in awe of the number of people, especially the older students. I was standing there, leaning on the staircase, admiring one of the $8^{th}$ grade couples and how grown-up they looked. Charlotte caught me staring at them and headed straight for me.

"LilyAnn, don't stare at them," she told me. "You are with me, and being with older kids is going to be common now. Just smile and act like you are the most confident, beautiful girl in the room, and you won't be nervous. Just don't think you are more beautiful than me," she giggled. How did she even know that was who I was looking at? She had some crazy superpowers, or I wasn't as discrete as I thought I was.

Ok. New plan.

Act confident. Got it.

Act beautiful. I think I got it.

Don't be nervous. I don't have that. I am going to work on that, though.

Just as I let out a sigh thinking this night was going to have too many rules to remember, I heard the doorbell ring. I instinctively looked over to the door and saw J.R. and Lucas walk in with a few more of their friends. I immediately smiled at them. Lucas and I made eye contact, and he smiled back at me. I watched him as he walked over to where I was standing.

"Hey, LilyAnn. You look nice."

"Thanks," was all I could say.

"I don't see you in dresses much." Lucas noticed. I blushed. I was amazed he noticed something like that.

Lucas and I kept talking until we heard the music stop. It was Charlotte's way of getting us to all listen to her instructions to go outside for a game she wanted everyone to play. The game wasn't an option. Everyone seemed to know that as they followed her lead to the backyard.

"OK, everyone! Listen up. I am going to explain the game. We are playing musical chairs but with a twist," Charlotte yelled. I was officially nervous. Lucas and I looked at each other and shrugged. We were not sure what was going to happen, but at least I felt like I had an ally.

Charlotte explained all the rules. Whoever got out each round had to say something negative about someone else who was still in the game. Some people laughed, thinking it was going to be funny. Some people looked nervous. Some just rolled their eyes, but no one left or said no. This was going to be a long night.

...

Soon enough, the game was going strong. People were getting knocked out and then saying crazy things about other people. Most just chose to say something about one of their good friends. I think they did that so they could easily apologize later. The comments were more embarrassing as opposed to mean. No one was really taking the game too seriously up to that point. I even found myself laughing alongside people as they told stories. I was smiling more than I thought I would have been playing one of Charlotte's crazy games.

We all started another round. The song that was playing seemed to go on forever. I had gone completely in a circle about five times, no make that six, no seven. Oh, my goodness, I was getting too dizzy to keep count. The song finally stopped, and people started diving onto chairs. Some people played dirty and pulled chairs away as someone was about to sit down, and some were holding onto their chairs for dear life. When all the commotion was over, Charlotte was the one who was out. Everyone started looking at each other. No one wanted to be on the other end of the comment she was about to make, and of course, she was going to be dramatic about it.

"Raegan." Charlotte cooed slowly as a sly smile started to appear.

Raegan covered her face to hide. Charlotte threw her head back and laughed.

"No. I will say LilyAnn instead."

Ouch. I looked around the backyard and then finally back at Charlotte. She continued, "LilyAnn, something negative about you is your old best friends. They are such goodie goodies and absolutely no fun. So glad you have dumped them," Charlotte professed as she took her Diet Pepsi and held it up to the sky for people to know it was time to cheer at what she had said. She looked at me and blew me a kiss. I think she was almost trying to compliment me. I was too stunned to start to walk as the next song started. I turned around and started to walk back into the house instead. My breathing got heavy as I searched the kitchen for a water bottle. I knew she could have said worse things about me, things that would have people judging me or looking at me differently. But she didn't. I didn't know if she said what she did because she wanted to hurt me and knew that was the way to do it or if she was just stating her truth. She thought my oldest friends were negative people weighing me down.

...

When the party was over, I decided to go home instead of sleeping over at Charlotte's. I needed some time to reflect on what happened tonight. There were some great moments, times when I enjoyed myself and felt on top of the world. There were times that I laughed with people, and my cheeks would hurt from smiling so much. There were other times, however, when I felt ashamed. I felt bad every time someone got out and had to say a negative thing about someone. You could see that some people struggled to do it. This game could do some serious damage to people's self-esteem. I assumed that was exactly what Charlotte intended.

Most of all, though, I was upset about what Charlotte said about Mae and Jordan. I had been missing them like crazy lately. To hear she thought my biggest negative was them was heartbreaking. Mae and Jordan were not my negative; they were my positive. My strength.

I picked up my phone and instinctively started to dial Mae's number. I want to tell her what I was thinking. Just as I hit the last number, I realized what I was doing. I hung up right away. I didn't know much after tonight, but I did know Mae wouldn't want to hear from me, especially about this. I threw my phone on the floor and started to cry.

...

Mae and Jordan were curled up on the couch, under a big, fluffy blanket, watching a scary movie. Mae looked over at Jordan and laughed as she put more M&Ms into the bowl of popcorn. Mae was grateful for a sleepover together tonight since most people they knew were going to be attending Charlotte's party. Mae and Jordan didn't care that they weren't invited – they had each other, and that was what was most important to them.

Suddenly, a scary part of the movie made them scream. Both girls jumped up, popcorn flying everywhere.

"Ahhh! LilyAnn, close your eyes. You'll get nightmares for sure!" Mae screamed and chuckled. She always reminded LilyAnn about her nightmares ever since they watched their first scary movie together in the 3$^{rd}$ grade. LilyAnn had had nightmares over one scene every night for weeks.

Just then, it got eerily quiet.

"I can't believe I said that," Mae whispered with tears in her eyes.

Jordan put her arm around her shoulder. "It's not just you. I thought of her during that part too." Jordan paused and then continued, "I miss her too."

Both girls sat in silence for a minute before the phone rang, making them both jump again and start giggling.

Mae picked it up quickly. "Hello. LilyAnn?" There was a pause while Jordan waited anxiously. "No. I am sorry. You have the wrong number." Click. Mae hung up.

Both girls smiled at each other and then turned their attention back to the movie. "I just thought, maybe," Mae said so quietly that Jordan wasn't sure if Mae really said it or if it was her imagination.

# CHAPTER 12

# COWARDS AND THE FEARLESS

That next Monday at school was not easy. It was the first day back to school after the party and was almost just as hard as the first day of middle school. The kids who were at the party looked like they were on edge a bit. They kept looking around as they walked down the hall. A couple were even absent. I guessed that was what happens when people share things about each other. I prayed this all would blow over by the end of the week. Party games were supposed to be fun, not have lingering negative effects for days.

Tuesday and Wednesday were the same. Go to school, observe what was going on between people, and try to stay out of drama. I tried to make eye contact with Mae and Jordan a few different times during these two days, but I wasn't successful. I sat back and noticed the way Charlotte was taking this opportunity to be more vocal since some kids were being more reserved. I noticed how she was being obnoxious every time Jessica seemed to be within earshot of her.

I was trying to stay out of drama. Generally, that looked like me being me, just more quiet than normal. I kept to myself a bit, I only half listened to what people were saying, and I kept my head down as I walked through the halls. This gave me the time I needed to think my own thoughts and reflect. I found myself thinking a lot about how this year had started.

I thought and reflected on all of this through the end of the week, and what stuck with me most by Friday were three revelations about people and popularity in general. First, I loved being considered popular. That was just true. Second, being popular came with a price. My price was high. It had cost me my favorite friendships with Mae and Jordan. Man, I missed them. And third, middle school was full of people that fell into two main categories: cowards and fearless.

I knew not everyone could be categorized as a coward or as fearless, but so many kids could be. I could tell by both the big and the small things they did.

I considered the situation I had found myself thinking about lately: Jessica. This drama created by Charlotte was getting out of control. Being mean seemed to be contagious. Poor Jessica was now getting made fun of by more people than just Charlotte. Don't make any mistake – Charlotte was still the ringleader.

But, because she did it, everyone thought it was cool and that they should do it too. People called her names behind her back; some said things to her face. Some people waved their hands in front of their noses when she walked by, while others taped things to her locker that they knew would upset her. Some people wrote nasty things on Post-Its and slapped them on her back. I'm amazed at what people thought was ok to do to someone and at how they didn't seem to feel guilty about it. I felt awful and guilty for just watching it all happen, and I wasn't even doing or saying any of the mean things. I started to think that I wasn't so sure when the kids I went to school with started to be so cruel to others.

...

I decided I needed a quiet space, somewhere Charlotte and Raegan wouldn't come looking for me. I headed to the library.

I walked towards the back of the library, to the last table in the corner that I found so peaceful. Even in the library, I was never alone. As I walked to the back, I passed tables of kids who were looking at me as I walked by. Some waved at me with hopeful smiles, some whispered, and some even made eye contact and then immediately turned their heads. It was a weird feeling to be noticed like that.

As I reached my favorite table, I took out my notebook and sat. I took a deep breath and opened it. I looked at everything I had been writing for the last few days. While I was organizing my theory on people either being cowards or being fearless, when Mae quietly sat down across from me. I was so deep in my thoughts I didn't even notice her.

I wrote that I think cowards are people who do things to hurt people, but they usually do it behind their backs. They enjoy the drama or even hurting someone's feelings, yet they don't put themselves out there when they attack someone. They may choose to stay behind the scenes because they are too embarrassed, or simply because they don't want to get caught. Cowards may write something on social media, leave notes somewhere, or talk to other people about someone. Cowards don't usually get caught doing these mean acts. There's not always proof that they did them. But the damage is still out there when they are done. Once it is said, or worse, posted, there is no way to take it back. Unfortunately, these tactics are both successful, as well as extremely harmful. I realized there were always several cowards around me.

Fearless people have no problem being mean to people. They say or do harmful things to people whenever they feel like it. They, too, like the drama, and being mean to others. When you are fearless, you also like the spotlight. Take some of the kids in my very own hallways at school. They will say unkind things loudly while walking amongst groups of people, just to hurt people's feelings. They do this in the hallways, classrooms, on the buses, and even at sporting events. They use their real names when they post on social media or write negative comments about others. They don't stress about what they are doing or the outcome of what they do. Some fearless people will even say whatever they want straight to someone's face. Some don't hide behind the screens. They almost take pride in being cruel, like it's an accomplishment of how creative and vindictive they can be. I was always amazed by this.

Although there is a big difference in how these two types of people interact with others, one thing is the same. They are thoughtless and cruel. They do damage that they don't even know about.

I paused, lost in my own thoughts, trying to think about how this related to Jessica. Now and then, I noticed someone who seemed to be upset when something happened to Jessica. I noticed they didn't seem to like what was going on either, but they were like me and didn't seem to be doing anything to stop what was happening at school. They watched quietly without saying anything. They turned their heads, pretending not to see what was going on around them. It bothered us, but we didn't do anything. Sometimes ignoring what was happening felt like the safe thing to do. But safe for who? Not for Jessica or other kids like her in school.

I was beginning to see that we, the people who watched but didn't do anything to help, were a problem too. We were not the bully, and we were not the victim. We were just the bystanders, literally watching terrible things happening to good people. That described me perfectly. I felt trapped by what was right and what I didn't want to give up.

As I contemplated this idea, I wrote faster. My brain was racing as I tried to put all these pieces together to make sense. I was a bystander. However, I was a coward, too – it just looked different than some people. I decided the best spot for me was my new, third group of people: the bystanders. It was for people who watch but for whatever reason, don't do the right thing. I hated that that was where I saw myself, but that was where I was.

...

"You almost look too serious to interrupt. I hope it's ok that I sat down," Mae quietly said to me. I was so startled I gasped. I put my hand to my chest, took a breath, put down my pen, and smiled at her. I guess I was pretty focused. She laughed at my reaction and then just watched me. I realized she was waiting for me to say that it's okay that she sat down.

"Are you kidding? Of course it is okay! I am glad you did. I was just trying to organize some things that have been swimming around in my head. Nothing that can't wait."

"Great!" She paused for what seemed like forever, but it was only about a minute. I just sat and waited until she was ready to continue.

"Listen, don't think I'm not still really mad at you. I am. I'm hurt too. But I want to check on you. Make sure you are doing alright."

"I know you are still mad and even hurt. I never meant to hurt you guys. I hope you know that," I said quietly as my eyes teared up. I truly meant what I was saying. My heart raced because our friendship used to be the easiest thing in the world. As I sat there waiting for her to respond, I realized how I had changed it. I felt both the stress and hope ooze out of me sitting there with her.

"I know you didn't mean to hurt us, but it happened just the same." She paused before going on, and I just looked at her with sympathy in my eyes as I waited for her to continue. "I don't want to harp on that, on what is happening between us. I just want to check in on you," Mae explained.

I looked hard at her, trying to figure out what she was asking me.

"Check in on me? That's sweet, but besides missing you guys, I'm doing great. I mean, middle school has been so much fun so far. Don't you think?" I had a question in my voice, and I could tell by the way she looked at me that she noticed it too.

"If you say so." Mae put her head down, and I watched her. I realized I may have tried to sell how great everything was going a bit too hard. I had just been writing down that I thought I was a problem, wasn't I?

Mae finally spoke up again.

"Middle school has been tougher than I expected. Kids are tougher than I expected. And to be honest, the hardest part is that I didn't plan on not talking to you every day. That is the part I don't like the most this year."

I contemplated her words.

"I know not talking is hard. I don't like it either. What else has made middle school harder than you thought it would be?" I questioned her. I knew I was pushing it since I had been playing such a huge role in her and Jordan not loving middle school. I almost felt bad that I asked her for more information. Before I could think too much about it, Mae looked up at me. She was staring at me with such intensity in her gaze.

"Kids are meaner than they were last year. I don't like the bullying that has been going on this year either. I especially don't like that you're a part of it," she explained quickly. Her voice changed as she spoke. It had a chill and a sadness to it. I wasn't sure if she caught it, but I did.

My eyes opened wildly, and I was looking at her, really looking at her. "I am not bullying anyone," I reassured Mae. I said it with just a hint of wavering in my voice.

Mae looked at me for a few seconds without saying anything and then stood up. "Aren't you, though?" was all she said before she walked out of the library.

I just stared off after her as if I was waiting to see if she was going to come back to say something else to me that would make more sense. But she didn't. She didn't even look back. This didn't surprise me.

At that moment, I wasn't sure what was worse – that she walked out after accusing me of being a part of the bullying or that she read my mind. I mean I was just thinking that I was a problem in some way. Didn't I just conclude that I was being a bystander? I was witnessing things happen but was too scared to act in any way. I shouldn't be surprised that Mae had it figured out already too. She knew me and knew this should be bothering me. The worst part was, she also knew I wasn't doing anything to stop it.

...

Later that afternoon, I found myself slowly walking towards PE. I stopped as soon as I saw the sign-up sheet for the middle school musical outside of the gym doors. I smiled, knowing I had been looking forward to trying out for the musical this year. It was the one place in my life I didn't mind the drama!

Since I had last period PE, I had the privilege of seeing everyone who had signed up earlier in the day. The list was full of people from all different cliques. I smiled at how cool that was to see. Some kids on the list I knew could sing, some I had no idea about, and some I didn't think could sing at all (but I thought it was awesome they were going to try!). I laughed to myself as I thought of how these auditions might go. Either way, I was still excited to see such a diverse group of people who were planning on auditioning. I read the information, grabbed the pen that was hanging off the bulletin board, and quickly signed my name. When I finished, I turned around and came face to face with someone waiting for me to finish. I jerked back for a second, surprised, and then smiled at her. Jessica was standing right behind me, waiting to get to the flier. She gave me a weak smile back, and I handed her the pen. As I moved out of the way for her, I thought, *This is going to be an interesting audition.* Jessica briefly looked over the list, sighed loudly to herself, hesitated, and then signed her name. She stared at the list for a minute after she signed her name, so I glanced at what she was staring at. I saw Charlotte and Raegan's names on the list. They each had a big star next to their names. A lightbulb went off in my head. Of course that would make her hesitate. It would make me hesitate if I were her too. I started to wonder if she would change her mind and cross her name off, but she didn't. She turned around, and we made eye contact. I had no idea why, but I was still just standing there.

It was one of those moments you knew was important, but had no idea why. I felt like she wanted to say something but decided not to. I felt like I should say or do something profound right then, but I didn't. Instead, I said, "Are you excited about the musical?"

Jessica just looked at me. The look in her eyes said so much. It held so much sadness and confusion. She gave me an awkward half grin and then nodded before turning and walking towards the gym. I didn't know how to react. Not knowing what to say or do, the next bell rang. I walked down the hall and headed into the girl's locker room.

...

As I walked into the locker room, I noticed a bunch of the girls giggling by their lockers. Some were whispering in small groups, and some were stopped in front of a locker. Jessica's locker. I knew in my gut nothing good was about to happen. I made my way over to see what was going on. There was a sign taped on Jessica's gym locker. The sign wasn't very creative or anything, but it was mean enough to make Jessica run into the bathroom stall with tears in her eyes. I felt awful for her. I looked back at that poster, at the star at the bottom, and I knew who put the poster there. So did everyone else. Fearless.

CHARLOTTE IS FEARLESS.

> ### THIS LOCKER IS HOME FOR ALL RMS RENTAL UNIFORMS
>
> Since Jessica will never be able to afford to buy her own.
>
> *

I stood in front of Jessica's locker for a while in shock and amazement. I shook my head and walked straight over to the bathroom stalls to look for her. I didn't know which one she was in until I heard a shaky sob. I put my hand on the stall door. I wanted to say something, to do something, but I just stood there frozen. I had no idea what to say. I heard the crying slow down and then stop. She was finally taking deep breaths. The stall opened, and I jumped back against the wall. Jessica walked right past me, straight out of the bathroom, and picked up a rental uniform from the office. She changed for class. I'm not sure if she even blinked. She didn't make eye contact with a single person. Before anyone even exhaled from holding their breath, she was out of the locker room.

As we lined up, I watched Jessica. Almost all the girls did. Some giggled and whispered more than normal, all while staring in her direction. Some girls looked more sympathetic than usual. I just stood there and observed all of them. I kept thinking about what just happened in the locker room. I couldn't stop the picture of Jessica running to the bathroom, upset, from replaying in my mind.

I wasn't paying too much attention to what was going on in class. All I knew was we were waiting to get picked for volleyball teams. As I was staring off into space, Lucas walked up behind me.

"Hey." He laughed as I jumped about two feet in the air.

"Hey." I weakly smiled back at him. "How are you?"

"It seems I'm doing better than you. You don't seem like yourself. I picked you for my team twice, and you never even walked over. I was going to tease you, but I could tell by your face you were upset."

"I'm sorry I'm not paying attention. Thanks for picking me. Twice." I looked at him and genuinely smiled. "Thanks for noticing I was upset." It felt good that someone noticed I had a lot going on in my head. Someone took time to notice me, and I was not even getting bullied or anything like that. It warmed my heart and yet made me feel guilty all at the same time.

"No problem. Are you ready to play?" He looked at me cautiously.

I smiled at him. "I'll be right there." I went to the water fountain, took a few sips, and splashed some water on my face. I needed to figure out what was going on in my head, but it wasn't going to be done in the middle of gym class. For now, I went to play volleyball.

I got home after school and took out my journal. I needed to process some of the things I had been thinking about from the day. I was thinking about how all of this was happening in school, a place that should be safe for all kids. It was crazy to me that Jessica hadn't told anyone anything yet. If she had, I hadn't noticed anything getting done or anyone getting in trouble. She may have been too shy to speak up, being new and all. However, I was surprised no one, not even one adult at school, had noticed all the little things that people were doing to her. There had been noticeable signs, hadn't there? There had been a literal paper sign! How did the PE teacher miss this? There had been other signs too. She talked even less than she did before, and that said a lot since she had never really talked a bunch. She was always walking with her head down too. No adult seemed to be picking up on those little things yet. I was hoping they would soon because if I was noticing, I felt like someone else should too.

The biggest problem I had with myself at that point was I knew I was just as bad as the adults who hadn't noticed anything yet. Honestly, I was probably worse. I was noticing all the changes in Jessica, and I was not saying anything out of fear for myself. I wasn't saying anything because I didn't want anyone to get mad at me. I was getting upset with myself, yet I knew I wasn't ready to say anything. I prayed someone noticed something soon so I wouldn't have to be the one to come forward! I was afraid of what would happen to Jessica if they didn't. Her personality was slowly starting to change, and not for the better.

I AM A BYSTANDER

I AM A WITNESS.

I AM SCARED.

# CHAPTER 13

# GAME ON

I found myself going through the motions at school. I stood by our lockers in the morning. I smiled when I was supposed to smile and laughed when other people laughed. I sat by Charlotte and Raegan at lunch. I complimented the things Charlotte said when I felt she wanted me to compliment them. It was a little weird to me that neither Charlotte nor Raegan felt like there was anything wrong with me. If they did notice, they hadn't said anything to me. I mean, I felt a little bit like a robot. My heart just wasn't with them. I realized I was going to have to start making some choices. I was going to have to start deciding what I stood for, and what I was passionate about. When I was with Mae and Jordan, we always talked about things like morals, standards, and passion. We would ask each other questions like what do we need to do to be great people? What should we be doing for others? What can we do that will help ensure people will remember us forever? I didn't always have the answers to those questions, but I liked to think that I still cared about trying to find them. I liked to believe we were having important conversations together. I was missing those kinds of chats. I was missing Mae and Jordan.

At lunch, I heard Charlotte and Raegan talking. I didn't listen to them, though. My mind was so far away from their basic chatter.

"What do you think, LilyAnn?" Charlotte asked me. I looked up and saw both of their faces staring at me. I blinked. They were still staring.

"Welllll," Raegan dragged out her question.

"I'm not sure. What do you guys think?"

They didn't answer me at first, and I started to think I was going to be in trouble with them for not paying attention. Suddenly, Charlotte started talking super-fast. She was taking that opportunity to tell me exactly what she thought about our math teacher. Poor man. He didn't know it, but he was now on her list as well.

I couldn't believe I got out of that situation. I needed to pay more attention to them, or they would think I wasn't interested in them. In that moment, I was about the worst person I could be. I was not a good friend to Mae and Jordan. I was not being a good person to Jessica. I was so preoccupied that I was not even being nice to Charlotte and Raegan. If I wasn't careful, I was going to end up alone.

...

A few days after the sign-up sheet for the school musical was posted, Charlotte and Raegan announced we needed to rehearse for our auditions. Apparently to them, it was imperative for our social standing that all three of us get cast in the musical. I walked down the hall towards the music room to meet them for our first practice. As I went, I couldn't help thinking how interesting this whole thing would be. I made the turn toward Mr. Hamill's classroom, and saw both Charlotte and Raegan's heads together. They had their ears up against the music room door.

Before I could utter a syllable to ask them what in the world they were doing, they put a finger over their lips, telling me to be quiet. They motioned for me to hurry up and get next to them. I started down the hallway towards the music room, Charlotte, and Raegan.

Before I even got to the door, I heard it. The most beautiful voice I had ever heard. I swore whoever was singing must have had a daily voice lesson her whole life and was only one audition away from winning The Voice next season. I was both mesmerized and a bit jealous of this captivating voice. I briefly closed my eyes and smiled as I appreciated the singing.

"What are you smiling about?" Raegan brought me back to attention with a loud whisper.

"I was just listening and admiring whoever is singing. I didn't know I was smiling." I explained it quickly to them both. "She is amazing. Who is in there?" I wanted to know.

At the same time, with the same disgust in their eyes, they both spit out, "Her!"

It took me a second to figure out who they were both so annoyed with. I mean, there was always a list. But there was only one person right now who would make both Charlotte and Raegan look like fools if she was better at them in anything:

Jessica.

Oh, and believe me, she was better. So, so, so much better.

"So, what is the plan?" Raegan demanded as she whisper-yelled at us. For being Charlotte's sidekick, she sure was getting just as bossy and nasty as Charlotte.

"Why does there have to be a plan?" I asked, although I knew the answer already. I also knew I was just trying to keep some peace.

"Are you serious? I'm going to assume you are joking, so I will continue. Of course, there is a plan. Or at least there will be one," she smirked. "I am concocting it up in my head as we speak. All I know is that before anyone else hears her, we will have to destroy her. She'll never utter a musical note, or any other note, in this school. She can't."

Raegan was giggling so loudly that she started quickly down the hallway with her hand covering her mouth to make sure no one heard. Charlotte strutted down slowly after her. I hung back, a little in shock about what just happened. I knew I shouldn't be, but sometimes I was still amazed at some of the things those two girls thought and said. I turned and looked through the window. Poor Jessica. All she was doing was singing. Singing and smiling. She finally looked happy. I don't think I had ever seen her smile. The scary part was, she had no idea what was about to happen to her. I didn't know for sure either, but I knew it was not going to be pretty.

The pit in my stomach was back with a vengeance. It was the same pit that I got every time I thought about what kind of friend I was being to Mae and Jordan; the same pit I got every time Jessica was involved or was a victim of one of Charlotte's plans. No good was going to come out of whatever happened next. I knew this, yet I was not sure I could stop it. I was not sure I was strong enough to stop it.

I took a deep breath and let it out. A skill I was getting pretty darn good at this year.

I started down the hallway to catch up with Charlotte and Raegan. I needed to learn what my part in Charlotte's plan was going to be. I was hoping I didn't have to do anything, or at least nothing directly. I didn't want to hurt Jessica. Yet with every step, I took down the hall, I knew they were going to involve me. I knew this, and I was walking toward them anyway. With every step, I was losing my strength. I was losing my ability to make good choices. I was losing myself.

This was my price for popularity.

...

It was like the universe knew I was at odds with myself. It was trying to keep me on my toes. The universe, or some other mystical force, kept throwing me scenarios that I must work through, make decisions about, and act to complete. Today was no different.

I was still sulking as we walked out of the music wing and headed outside. As the door to the school closed behind us, I saw a glimpse of my old life, what my life could have been now if I had just made the other choice. Mae and Jordan sat on the benches just outside of school with a couple of girls we sometimes liked to hang with. They were in a moment of true bliss. I smelled candy, lots of sugar, and cinnamon scents that filled the air around them like a delicious cloud. I heard laughter, a lot of laughter. The kind where their bellies hurt after because they were laughing so hard. I saw smiles. I saw joy. I saw my friends and their ability to feel good.

I was so envious of them in that moment. As I walked away, the sounds of laughter died, and the sounds of anger, fretting, and manipulation started to take their place. These sounds did not fill me up the way the other ones did. Still, I continued to follow those sounds all the way to Charlotte's house.

...

Charlotte threw herself on her bed and screamed, "We need better ideas!"

I was not sure what to say since she was the only one coming up with any ideas.

"What will make her so mortified it won't matter that she can sing. She won't ever want to sing?"

As she was asking this question, she was simultaneously looking through the latest copy of Vogue magazine. I found this whole scene to practically be right out of the movie *Mean Girls*. The problem was I didn't fully understand why I hadn't stood up and left yet. I knew I wasn't mean, but I was not being very nice either. If I didn't say something soon, they were going to think I was weak, but if I said something to hurt Jessica, I wouldn't be able to live with myself. Ugh!

Raegan finally spoke up.

"OK, let's think about what we have been doing all year. We have been going after her clothes or really, lack of them. Why don't we continue that? We make people laugh all the time in class."

Charlotte jumped off the bed and tackled Raegan. She was talking so fast that I could barely keep up. What I did understand I knew was bad. I heard laughter, more kids, and ideas. Most importantly, I heard the words "social" and "media."

We were going ahead with this plan. I was sick to my stomach.

"Genius!" Charlotte said to herself. She finally stopped talking and stood straight up. We were all in this together, and I knew our next play. The gleam in her eyes bore right into my soul, although I'm not even sure I had one left anymore. I knew I was in for trouble, and if I was in trouble, poor Jessica wasn't going to know what hit her.

# CHAPTER 14

# LET THE PLAN BEGIN

Charlotte demanded we get on social media and, more importantly, go viral. We would start by making a video and then sending it to everyone we knew. Social media could do so much damage. I knew this was going to be bad. But since Charlotte was fearless, nothing was going to change her mind.

The plan was pretty basic. However, since it was coming from Charlotte, it would be viewed, valued, and most importantly for her, shared. She was going to take Jessica's face and add it to a video with someone else's voice. The voice Charlotte had picked sounded awful – incredibly off-pitch and whiny. They were also putting a picture of a garbage dumpster behind her face with the logo 'DUMPSTERS R US' on it to make sure everyone remembered they were still supposed to be making fun of her clothes. Charlotte and Raegan were convinced this was going to be a hysterical way to mortify her. I was sure it would mortify her. I couldn't help thinking how terrible this idea was and what Jordan and Mae would think of me after this was posted on social media. Even though I wasn't helping to make the video, I knew it would still be a reflection on me. I was suddenly so sick to my stomach that I needed to get up. I started to gather my things, but before I could make up an excuse to leave the house, the computer was open, and Charlotte had started typing away as she talked to each of us. It was too late to casually leave. I was stuck there to witness the whole thing.

"Ok, ladies, here we go." Charlotte connected her iPhone to her computer and pulled up a video of Jessica singing.

"Ummm, Charlotte. Where did you get that video?" I was almost scared to hear her response. Taking pictures or videos of kids in school without their permission was not allowed. Of course, that had never stopped Charlotte.

"I videoed her in the music room the other day after we discovered she can sing. I figured it couldn't hurt to have some footage of her for something; I just didn't know what I'd use it for when I recorded it. The fact that I have it on my phone has been bothering me since it is evidence that she is good and all. I almost deleted it just because of that. I am so glad I kept it. It is coming in handy for the video we are making. To be honest, I almost forgot about it until Raegan mentioned we can still make fun of her clothes. It all came rushing back to me because I was laughing so hard when I noticed her socks with her skirt that day. So gross." Charlotte continued typing away while she talked to us. She didn't let us respond to anything she was saying. She was just at her computer playing with the video that I knew would haunt Jessica like it was the most natural thing in the world for her to be doing right now.

As Charlotte edited the video, Jessica's voice played for a few quick seconds. It sounded beautiful, so light and happy. Tears immediately stung my eyes. I got up from the floor, ran to the bathroom, and quickly shut the door. I couldn't bear to watch what would happen next. I just knew they were going to make sure Jessica sounded like a dying chicken — a poor, loud, squawking, dying chicken. I didn't open the door to go back into the bedroom. I stayed in the bathroom staring at myself in the mirror. I didn't go out there and tell them to stop. I didn't go out there and tell them they were being mean. I didn't go out there to leave. I just plain didn't go out there.

I was worse than a coward.

...

"Annnnd done! It is officially posted on Instagram. We are so going to become social media famous… Or at least Jessica will!" Charlotte laughed wickedly. The gleam in her eyes was honestly kind of scary.

Within minutes, I mean less than 3 minutes, the video had over 250 views. Charlotte was dancing around her bedroom, loudly shrieking about the possibility of going viral. Viral. I prayed that the people looking at the video would all be local kids who were only quick to respond because it was Charlotte's account. Eventually, it would die down. Right?

The conversation quickly moved to talking about the comments. Oh, the comments. They were coming in fast. Loud and fast. Most of the comments were funny, just enjoying the video for what it looked like – a video some kids made to be funny. However, some of the comments were mean. I mean really, really mean.

Most of the comments were about how Jessica must not be able to sing or how they couldn't believe someone with that awful of a voice thought it was a good idea to sing at all.

Some of the comments are about what she was wearing. They talked about how Jessica's outfit was outdated, that it didn't fit her, and the overall bad state that her clothes were in. What was so heartbreaking to me were those comments, because the clothes in the video were her real clothes. They didn't photoshop them. The comments just fueled Charlotte and Raegan to get more amped up. The comments were like little pieces of affirmation that they could use to continue to move forward with their plan to take her down. They decided it would be a great idea to make another video. They were laughing so hard, saying that another video must be done, and now. I needed to get out of there – it couldn't happen soon enough!

"Hey guys, I just saw the time. I promised my mom that I would be home by now. I'm sorry, I need to take off now."

"Really, LilyAnn? We are just getting started! The next stop is Snapchat and maybe YouTube. Wait until you see what we are posting. It's going to be so good it might even make her mom cry!" Raegan excitedly exclaimed.

"Yeah, super sorry I have to miss that." I drew out the words as I rolled my eyes a bit. "I'll have to see the video later on and you guys tomorrow morning." I started to pack up my things as quickly as possible and head to the bedroom door. As I did, I turned around to look at them. They were already prepping for the second video. I was out of sight, out of mind. They were going full steam ahead. I stood at the door for a couple of minutes, trying to hear what the plan was, trying to prepare myself. If I heard them right, this video was going to be Jessica with a background. I listened a little harder. They were trying to figure out how to alter her actual face to make her look like an animal living by a dumpster. They also wanted to add a second animal to be her mom saying mean things to her. I gasped, and my hands flew to my mouth. I turned around and ran out. As I walked out and shut the door to Charlotte's house, I realized a tear was rolling down my face. I wiped it away and tried to catch my breath. I couldn't though.

I was only in the bedroom with them. I didn't have any part in what happened or what was about to happen. Right? I didn't record Jessica or even help make the videos of her. I never put my hands on the computer, and I never uploaded anything to social media. I can't be blamed at all, right? I tried to reason with myself as I ran home. I tried to envision a universe where someone would agree that I was innocent in this current debacle. I pondered this until I got to my street.

As I walked down my sidewalk, I slowed down. My chest felt like it was going to explode. My stomach was in knots as it was flipping over and over. Somehow, deep down, I knew I was wrong. I knew I was also to blame for what was happening to Jessica right now.

I cried the rest of the way home.

...

I walked up the stairs to my front door. However, I couldn't open the door to go inside. Not yet. I feared that once I walked into my room, I would continue to judge myself. Judge who I was becoming and the choices I kept making. I couldn't do that in my room just yet. My room has always been my safe space. A room with sweet memories. A room that brought me joy and even some independence. My room with pictures of my old friends who I'd neglected, yet who continued to shape me. Pictures of my new friends who had given me a shot of popularity. The same new friends who were being so cruel right now. A room with lessons written on my door, which I knew I hadn't read or followed in some time. All these thoughts crushed me. I took my hand off the doorknob and turned around. I put my back up against the front door of the house and slid down. I pulled my knees up to my chest and wrapped my arms around them. I leaned my head forward and tried again to catch my breath.

As I sat there on my front porch, I felt as lonely as I had ever felt. My ears perked up as I heard voices walking up the street.

"I can't believe those videos! They are so awful. Poor Jessica. If she doesn't see them tonight, tomorrow is going to be even worse. All the kids will be talking about it." Mae's voice drifted through the air and up to my porch.

"I know," Mae agreed. In a softer voice than she just used, she asked Jordan, "Do you think... Do you think LilyAnn had anything to do with the videos? Charlotte did tag her."

I sat listening to the voices get closer and closer to where I was sitting on my front porch.

"I would love to say no, that she would never do anything so petty or mean, but I don't know anymore. It is hard to say since she has been so off lately. I mean, I never thought she would stop talking to us, yet here we are now," Mae responded.

"I know, right?" Jordan huffed.

As I sat there, I could hear her annoyance with me. I could also hear that they were really getting close to my house now. I started to panic. I couldn't see them right now. I couldn't explain to them what had just happened at Charlotte's, especially since I didn't fully understand my part in it yet. I reached up, grabbed the doorknob, and twisted it, rolling backward into the entryway before quickly shutting the door.

Stop talking to them? That was what they thought I did. That was not what I was doing, though, was it? I mean, I tried to talk to them, but it was hard to balance all the things I had going on. It was hard to find the time, was all. Wasn't it? Ugh. I needed to go to bed. I needed to close my eyes and pray for my dreams to take me somewhere beautiful with a lot less drama and stomach-flipping.

I needed to rest.

Tomorrow was going to be a long day.

An incredibly long day.

## CHAPTER 15

# ALL THE ATTENTION

The attention. The attention that I was getting at school the next morning was making my guilt feel like it was 10 times worse than when I woke up. I didn't even think that was possible, but here I was. I was constantly looking around as we stood by our lockers. I swore it seemed like every student in the school stopped by to say something to us. It amazed me that so many people were coming up to us to tell us what a good job we had done. Most of the kids talked about how the videos were super funny. They even mentioned things about us being creative. What?!? I couldn't believe it.

I felt better each time someone walked by and said that the videos were not cool or that they didn't find them funny. The students who had enough courage to say anything didn't stop or say it to our faces, but I heard them as they walked by. At least they were doing that. I knew it was not a lot, but my faith in humanity grew a little each time I heard someone say something that Charlotte and Raegan wouldn't like if they heard it themselves.

I snapped back to the present as I saw JR and Lucas walking up to us. I couldn't pinpoint why I didn't want Lucas to say he liked the videos or that he laughed so hard at them. I offered a small smile and waited for them to give us their opinions.

"You guys killed those videos! When did you get so tech-savvy?" JR asked as he approached our lockers. "I watched them both about seventeen times." He put his arm around Charlotte as he turned and smiled at all of us.

Charlotte was beaming. She was loving the attention and praise. I noticed that Lucas didn't say they were funny or anything like that. My heart filled with a little bit of hope.

"I won't lie; they were creative. How did you come up with those ideas?" Lucas asked as he settled into the group circle. We made eye contact, and he rested his elbow on my shoulder. "I'm not sure if I ever would have been able to come up with that stuff."

"That is probably a good thing," I whispered under my breath.

Lucas looked at me right away and eyed me with suspicion. Nuts. I shouldn't have said that out loud. On the other hand, I felt like he heard me, I mean really heard me, and might have just understood what I was thinking. If he did, he didn't say anything, just like me. What passed between us was kind of our own little secret. His understanding reminded me people are human, and there may be more bystanders than I realized in this whole social game that was being played. I wished I could be as honest about my feelings with Mae and Jordan right now as I was with Lucas. For whatever reason, he tended to see the times I was in doubt over all that was happening. Maybe he would have some faith in me.

As I was pondering all these thoughts, the area around our lockers became the busiest it had been all morning. Since JR and Lucas kept standing by us, a ton of other boys did too. It stayed like this the rest of the morning.

Just when I started to relax and enjoy all the attention, the bell rang, and we were all off to class. It was going to get crazier as the day went on. I prayed I would get a fever before lunch so I could go home.

...

At lunch, Mae and Jordan looked like they were doing something they had never done before. They started walking towards the lunch table where I had been sitting with Charlotte and Raegan since I stopped sitting with them. As they got closer, my heart skipped, and then that pit in my stomach that never really went away since the first day of school doubled. I couldn't focus on anything but them walking.

"LilyAnn!" Charlotte exclaimed. "Are you even listening to me?" Her harsh tone brought my gaze from my oldest friends to my new friends.

"Sorry", I choked out. "I was just watching Jordan and Mae. They are coming over here."

"Ugh. What do they want?" Raegan muttered the question as Charlotte glared at them. Before I could even say anything, they both offered Charlotte and Raegan huge, fake, dazzling smiles. It caught me so off guard that I let out a small giggle.

"We are so glad you guys have so much to smile and laugh about today. It must be great to be you," Mae accused loudly. Her words had such a bite in her tone I didn't even respond. I was not strong enough to respond. They felt so bad for Jessica. They didn't think we cared, only that it was funny. But I did care. I so cared! But I found myself still silent.

"It is great to be us," Raegan chirped back at them. She didn't seem to notice the sarcasm in their tone. If she did, she ignored it. Probably since she truly did think it was great to be her. To be us. Without thinking, I rolled my eyes at Raegan but then stopped. I immediately started to pray that Charlotte didn't see me roll my eyes at Raegan.

"Whatever do you mean?" Charlotte batted her eyes innocently and put her hands under her chin as she blinked up at Mae. "We haven't done anything." She was definitely more clever than Raegan when dealing with sarcasm.

Mae and Jordan both rolled their eyes so hard I was sure they'd get a headache.

"You might think today is a victory for you, but it isn't. Not everyone thinks you are as funny as you do." Jordan snapped as they turned and walked away. My eyes followed them to see if they would turn around and look at me, but they didn't. They just kept on walking right out of the cafeteria.

If I had thought that encounter would rattle either Charlotte or Raegan, I was so wrong. Charlotte just popped her Diet Coke open as she watched the cafeteria doors close behind them. Her smile was freakishly huge. Charlotte and Raegan kept talking through lunch, while I only half listened. My mind was wandering in so many different places and directions. I was thinking about all the times Mae, Jordan and I used to talk about how being kind is so important. Important to us and important to the world. We would talk about how horrible it is to be mean to people, especially when there is no reason. As I reflected, I remembered that we also talked about how fun it would be to be popular. How great middle school would be if we had a larger group of friends to go to games with, to parties with, to school events with. Now here I was, and I couldn't tell if any of it felt worth it, especially without them.

Before I knew it, lunch was over.

Great.

It was time for English.

...

I walked out of the cafeteria in a daze. I started to walk down the hall, and Charlotte yelled at me to wait for her. I slowed down so she could catch up. She didn't look happy that I had left for English without her. I acted as if I thought she was right next to me and apologized to her. What I didn't tell her was that I was hoping to walk into that class without her this one time, but I wasn't that lucky.

I opened the door to class and walked in. I quickly got to my seat, put my stuff down, and sank into my chair. The sooner this class was over, the better. Right before class was about to start, the door opened. It was Jessica.

All I could think was, You're b*rave for coming to this class, Jessica. So brave.*

Jessica walked into class with red, puffy eyes. Her eyes and her facial expression said it all. My heart sank lower than I thought possible. She looked worse than I imagined she might. She whispered something to Mrs. Eachum and walked to sit in a different chair than she had been. She was going to sit next to Mae, who smiled warmly at her as she approached. As she walked to her seat, two things happened at once. Some kids were trying not to laugh out loud but were failing, and others were making comments about her singing and the videos loud enough for her to hear. Charlotte, of course, was the ringleader of all the comments. I couldn't even look in her direction. Mae looked over at me with a look in her eyes that I couldn't quite explain. It was one full of so many emotions that it was hard to digest. It was disgust, pain, disappointment, anger, and sadness all rolled into one look. I turned my head in shame. Although I couldn't look at her, I was grateful that she was sitting near Jessica this period. Grateful because Jessica now had an ally and (selfishly) grateful because it will distract Mae from giving me the evil eye all through class. I stared down at my paper and pretended to jot down some notes as Mrs. Eachum began class.

...

"LilyAnn! OMG, why aren't you listening this afternoon?" Charlotte screeched at me as we walked down the hallway.

"I am," I stuttered as I jumped to attention.

"So, of course, you agree then, right?" Her eyes were ogling me without even blinking as she awaited my answer.

"Of course," I slowly huffed out.

Charlotte responded to my agreement with a sparkling smile. Oh no, this was not going to be good. I was not sure what just happened or what I just agreed to. I started looking back and forth between them to see if I would learn something about what they had been talking about and what the plan would be.

However hard I tried to listen to them, I found my mind drifting from them again. I found myself wondering what Mae and Jordan were doing at that moment. I was so impressed that they were trying to address what was happening with Charlotte, Raegan, and Jessica. They spoke up today and said something to Charlotte and Raegan for Jessica. I didn't. I don't know if any other student was there for her today or if any adult had figured anything out yet, but at least Jessica had Mae and Jordan sticking up for her.

How could so much mischief be going on at school with no one else interfering?

I thought about what would be happening in school if teachers or administration knew anything. I felt like the teachers might talk to classes about bullying, being kind, or even proper social media use. Maybe there would be an all-school assembly. But none of these things were happening. We were all still being bystanders. I couldn't shake the feeling that we were all doing something so wrong, even if we were not actually doing anything at all.

...

The rest of the afternoon was a blur. I knew after school I was going to figure out what Charlotte and Raegan were talking about in the hallway. With the way they had been snickering all day, I was getting more nervous by the minute. As the last bell rang, and I stepped into the hallway, Charlotte grabbed my arm and started to hustle me down the hall. Raegan was right on our tail. They were practically skipping. They seemed so happy to be out of school and getting ready to start the next plan for Jessica.

I paid better attention this time to what they said. I listened to Charlotte and Raegan talk about going on a shopping trip. That seemed average enough. However, the more I heard, the more I got nauseous. This wasn't an average shopping trip; this trip was the main plan to humiliate Jessica. I couldn't say a word – I didn't say a word. I seemed to be living in a state of denial.

When did I become this person? When did being popular begin to mean more to me than being a good person? How could I go through with anything they were planning?

I finally tried to bring up the topic of doing something right, or at least not doing something totally evil.

"Hey, guys. I am just thinking. Is doing all these things to Jessica the right thing to do? Do we need to complete this next step of our plan? She is already mortified and humiliated."

There was no answer at first from either of them. Their silence caused me to open my eyes. Huh, I didn't even know when I shut them. They were looking at me like I was an alien. They seemed confused by my question before the confusion started to change to. To what? Anger maybe? Charlotte popped off the floor of her bedroom, and her finger got ready to point at me for a lecture.

Before she got the chance, though, I quickly continued: "I mean, is it going to make a difference? She might still decide to audition for the musical. If that happens, then, everyone is going to know she can sing. The videos and posts won't matter anyway."

"Ugh. Pay attention LilyAnn. The videos are just the start of our plan. Those are intended to rattle her self-confidence. We know she might still audition now, but hopefully, she will decide not to when we are done. We are going through with step two to make sure she is so embarrassed she won't do anything that puts her in the spotlight, ever. That includes auditioning for anything, a school musical or a choir solo. Nothing. We can't have her audition and let anyone hear that she is good at something. That is why we must be diligent and continue with our plans. We are doing the awful matching outfits from Goodwill. We are going to be wearing signs that will embarrass her. I don't want to hear that you doubt any of our ideas for this. You are with us now. The three of us always need to agree and do everything together. It is what our clique is expected to do. And we will do it well."

Charlotte took a breath and tried to calm herself. I just stared at her. She composed herself quickly and was already back to looking smug and impressed with her idea. She looked determined to win this game she was creating. She looked fierce, and it was almost scary. Now I wasn't only worried about not being in the popular group one day, but I was also worried about ever crossing her too.

# CHAPTER 16

# THE DAY I LOST MY SOUL AND FOUND IT

Two days ago, I made a deal with two devils.

Two days ago, I listened to Charlotte and Raegan go over all the details of our plan.

Two days ago, we went to Goodwill and the Twice is Nice store in our neighborhood to buy matching outfits. These outfits were thought out and designed to look like the perfect combination of poor and dirty, yet slightly chic since we were going to wear them. Charlotte concluded that the outfits we picked out and bought still looked cute on us.

Two days ago, I temporarily lost my soul and agreed to wear these outfits as a trio to finish the 'Take Down Jessica Plan.'

I sure hoped my soul was somewhere with Jordan or Mae because it certainly wasn't with me or Charlotte or Raegan.

Before school, and before I took part in this madness, I found myself needing to reflect. I jumped out of bed and grabbed my journal from my nightstand. It had been so long since I had taken the time to write in it. I held it in my hands and tried to think why I hadn't written in so long. I wondered if it was because I hadn't loved what I'd been doing lately, and I wouldn't want to reread all these events later. I wondered if it was because so many entries had included Mae and Jordan, and they hadn't been present recently. I was not sure of the reason, but I felt differently at that moment. I grabbed a pen from my dresser and plopped myself onto my bed. I opened the journal and wrote the date on the top. I paused with my pen over the page, smiled slightly, and then began.

I started my entry in the same way I had started all my entries since I began journaling: *Hey LilyAnn, it's me. Let's talk about what is going on.*

I wrote and wrote and wrote. I wrote about everything that had happened since that infamous day at the pool over the summer. I wrote about everything I had been doing and even all the things I hadn't been doing but should've been. I made sure to end with what we were doing that day. I wanted to make sure that when I looked back at this day – when anyone looked back at it – they knew I was sick to my stomach about doing it. I wanted to make sure I was writing about how conflicted I was. I knew that I was going to still go through with the plan simply because I did not know how or where to find the courage not to, but I wanted it on record somewhere that I was struggling. I was not excited to do this.

I closed the journal and then my eyes. The longer I paused, the lower I felt. I thought about Jessica and wondered how in the world she was doing. Of course, she was struggling too. Hers was not voluntary, though; someone was doing this to her.

We were doing this to her. I was doing this to her.

As I lay on my bed, time slowly passed. Before I curled up into a ball with all my blankets, I heard my mom yell up from downstairs. She was letting me know I was going to be late for school if I didn't get moving. Reluctantly, I got out of bed to face the day.

...

I slowly walked over to the hook that had the clothes laid out for today and methodically put on my outfit. I cringed as I put on my scratchy, pasty, beige turtleneck that had just the right amount of discoloration, stains, and small tears to make me look awful and sad. I did add a cute colored collar that made my eyes pop though, or at least that is what Raegan told me it did to make buying it worth it. I slipped into the long, plaid skirt that was frayed at the bottom and had paint splashed up one side. I attached a safety pin to the back to make sure it stayed on my hips since the skirt was at least two sizes too big. I finished off my specially created look by putting on old, dirty gym shoes. The sole was even coming off one of the shoes I put on. We had all bought similar pairs for the day. We would each have our hair in high, messy ponytails. 'Messy' was the keyword with this hairdo. I put mine up and stared in the mirror. My eyes betrayed me.

The look was complete. It matched the picture Charlotte sent to Raegan and me last night perfectly. The plan was we were going to all wear these similar outfits to school to mock poor Jessica. We were going to put signs on our backs that said mean things to poke fun at her. I was not even sure what they would say, but since Charlotte was making them, I was sure it would be nasty and personal. There would be filming. Lots of phones out and videoing. There would also be posting and all the things that came along with social media, including the comments. Charlotte already had comments created to put under the videos that got uploaded. Criminal. This plan was going to make the movie Mean Girls wish it had this scene in it. On paper, it sounded like we had a solid plan ready to go, right down to the hairdo, but all I wanted to do was throw up.

...

My mom peeked her head into my room to say good morning. She started to talk but stopped mid-sentence. She just eyed me up and down. She looked like she was taking it all in and was not sure how to proceed.

"So, what do we have here? A new fashion statement?"

"It's just a thing for today, mom. It's not a new statement. It's no big deal," I responded, talking quicker than I meant to. She knew I talked fast when I was nervous or excited.

"Are you sure? You look like it is a big deal. You look like you put a lot of time and effort into making this look, this 'thing', exactly right."

I didn't say anything; I just looked at her. I knew she wasn't done yet.

She continued, "Unless you are doing a school project that I am not aware of, I want you to make sure you are doing the right thing by walking out of the house looking like this. If you are not sure about yourself, then I would like you to open your closet door and read your lessons. Maybe that will help you determine your next move."

I quickly glanced at the closet and then back at my bedroom door. And just like that, as quickly as she came in, she left. She left me to think about what I should do next. I didn't want to open the closet; I knew what would happen if I did. However, if I didn't, I knew how I would feel. I slowly walked over to the closet and opened the door. My hand instinctively ran over all the words I had written over the years. I took a deep breath again and started to read all the lessons I had written in Sharpie.

LESSONS LEARNED

1. NEVER PUT A SQUARE PEG IN A ROUND HOLE

2. ALWAYS BE KIND

3. ALWAYS TELL THE TRUTH (you'll get in less trouble)

4. DON'T FORGET TO HAVE GOOD SPORTSMANSHIP

5. TRY TO SEE THE BEST IN OTHERS

6. BE KIND: NO BULLYING

7. SCHOOL IS HARD, FAMILY IS HARD, & SOMETIMES FRIENDSHIPS ARE THE HARDEST

8. ALWAYS REMEMBER TO BE A SQUARE PEG IN A WORLD OF ROUND HOLES

As soon as I started to read the title, I got teary-eyed. By the time I read lesson two, I was crying. By the time I read my last lesson, I knew I couldn't go to school wearing this outfit. I couldn't go through with this plan. I needed to do something else. I reread lesson eight. I remembered why I wrote it. I was feeling more confident as I remembered.

I needed to break the popularity rules. I needed to play a different game, even if I might not like what happened afterward. I needed to play my favorite game from kindergarten. I needed to be the square peg amongst all the round holes that had been surrounding me.

My mind was racing. I thought about the day I was in the library writing down the differences between people in middle school. The cowards, the fearless, and the bystanders. The cowards were the people who make fun of people behind people's backs, the ones who give in to peer pressure.

That reminded me a lot of Raegan.

The fearless were the people who would make fun of you right to your face. They are mean and don't care, especially if it gets them what they want.

That fit Charlotte perfectly.

I knew I had put myself in the bystander column, along with all the witnesses and people too afraid to act.

However, I started to think I needed a fourth and final group. The square peg group. The people who act and who do things differently group. They are the people who don't make fun of people because it is not kind. They are the ones who will stick up for people who have a tough time sticking up for themselves. The square pegs are unique, and like that, they don't fit the mold that people tell them they are in. They want to be themselves. Kind. Caring. Fun.

Mae and Jordan were square pegs.

I wanted to be a square peg too.

If being a square peg meant I would not be in the most popular clique, I was okay with that. I needed to start remembering my roots. I needed to remember that I had always been a square peg. I was okay with being different if that meant something positive happened.

I was a square peg among round holes. I needed to do some hammering!

My confidence was finally soaring. I felt more empowered than I had in weeks, maybe longer. I stood there in my beige, frumpy outfit and thought about what I could do to start to make all my wrongs right. I needed to come up with a plan of my own – it had to be successful and it had to be immediately! I fell to the floor and put my head in my hands. *Think LilyAnn, think.* I kept saying those words to myself as I pondered my next move.

...

A few minutes later, I had a plan, well, sort of. More like I had strength and needed to come up with a plan that others could get behind. Before I did anything, I knew what I needed to do first. I needed to call the only two people in the whole world I could tell this idea to: Mae and Jordan. I just prayed they would listen to me and come over. I was going to need some help! I slowly made it over to my phone and picked it up. I dialed a number I had dialed countless times before and waited while the phone rang and rang. I prayed she would answer my call, and just as I started to think she wouldn't, she did. The phone had stopped ringing, but there was no voice on the other line. She was waiting for me to say something first.

I took a deep breath and said, "Hello, Mae. It's me. Please don't hang up. Whatever you do, please don't hang up. You don't have to say a word. Just please listen to me. It is so important that you do."

I paused after my last words, waiting for a sign to continue. When I didn't hear the dial tone, I knew she was still there and not going to hang up. I took that as a good sign and continued.

"I know I have done nothing so far this school year to earn your trust or the right to ask for help, but here I am asking for it. Before you tell me no or all the reasons why I don't have the right to ask you for anything, please know that I am aware that I have been the biggest of brats. Please know, that I know, I need to make up for a lot of things. I am starting today, but I need your help. Before I can work on us, I need to help Jessica. I can't be a bystander anymore. I need to take some action to help Jessica. Can you please help me? Help me stand up for people and for all the mean things that have been happening to Jessica and that is going to continue to happen to her today. If you are willing, I need you to come over before school."

I said everything so quickly I hoped she understood what I was asking. My heart was racing as I waited for some kind of response from her.

There was a long pause. I just waited.

Finally, she said, "Jordan and I will be there in 10 minutes. Don't leave for school." And then she hung up.

Although hearing the dial tone made the pit in my stomach return, I considered this a huge win. She was coming, and she was bringing Jordan. We may have had a lot of work to do, but deep down, as always, I could count on my friends to be there for me.

As I waited, I paced.

Eight minutes later, both Mae and Jordan were at my front door. I could hear my mom answering the door. She was greeting them both with loud hellos and huge hugs. She also thought it had been a long time since we all hung out too. I listened as they walked up the stairs and down the hall to my room. Their steps stopped just outside my door.

I stopped pacing and waited.

They finally opened my door. I saw their expressions as soon as they stepped into my room and saw what I was wearing. Before they could say one word, and I knew they both wanted to say something, I did it first.

"I know, I know. This looks bad, and you have questions."

"Ummm, yes, it looks bad, and yes, we have questions," Jordan said as she looked at me with disappointment in her eyes. "Please tell me it is not what it looks like."

"It might be," I confessed. "I guess it depends on what you are thinking. If you are thinking that it looks like Charlotte came up with a plan for us all to wear these horrible outfits as part of a scheme to hurt Jessica and break her down so she doesn't audition for the musical, then you would be correct." I shrugged my shoulders and wiped away the tears that had made it to the bottom of my face. Crazy. I didn't even know when I started to cry.

"Well, that is exactly what I was thinking, and it is so awful!" Jordan cried. "However, seeing your tears helps me believe you are still part human." I sighed loudly when I heard her words, and a slow smile started to grow on her face.

Mae just stared at me for a minute. Before she said a word, she took a step closer to me and touched my outfit, putting her finger through a hole in my sweater. That one movement from her, that one action, broke my heart. I saw all the disappointment, worry, and even concern in her eyes as she looked up at me.

"I'm hoping you have an idea to stop this insane plan."

"Not exactly," I confessed. "Step one was getting you both here with me. I knew if I had you two next to me to help me, then we could come up with something. That was as far as I got so far. What are you thinking? Any ideas?"

Mae walked over to my closet door that I still had open. She ran her fingers over my handwritten lessons. She paused when she got to the bottom of the list. Without taking her hand off the list, she turned to face Jordan and me. A slow smile started at the corners of her lips.

"Well, okay then. Are you ready to get out your hammer?"

I nodded. "I sure am!"

And I meant it. I meant business. No more being a bystander. It's not the right thing to do. I was going to start making a difference, for Jessica, for my friends, and myself.

# CHAPTER 17

# HERE WE GO

It was great to have Mae and Jordan on my side again, brainstorming and working together. My heart was getting fuller by the second.

"So, before we can come up with an effective plan, we need to know as much as we can about what exactly has gone down so far. Please take it from the top and explain in five minutes or less." Jordan smiled at me.

"Okay, so you know about the videos on YouTube, Instagram, and Snapchat. Charlotte started with just the videos. When she got a lot of views, she tried to keep the momentum of the videos going by writing a lot of the mean comments that go along with the posts herself. The posts are not only mean, but they are also mostly lies, especially the ones about her singing. We heard her in the choir room the day the first video was posted. She was amazing. I mean, like, she has the best voice I have ever heard, kind of good. Charlotte and Raegan were insanely jealous and worried about the audition. They felt we had to be the ones to get the main parts in the musical, and that would never happen when Jessica's voice got out. No way. So, that day the videos were created and posted everywhere. They figured people had been right alongside them making fun of what she wore and about having to rent gym clothes every day etc., and people would get behind them on this. And they did. I mean, not everyone, but a lot. A scary amount. Not everyone was bold about it, but you can tell by what they were writing online and how they treated her in person at school that they would follow Charlotte's lead."

I began with this information. We spent the next 3 minutes just asking and answering questions.

It was a lot of information to have to go over and process. After it all was discussed, we moved on to thinking about what we could do to change the plan that was already in motion for that day.

"What are we missing about today, LilyAnn?" Mae asked.

A light bulb went off in my head, and I sprang up.

"Today is not just about the outfits. Charlotte is going to play clips of Jessica singing over the loudspeaker. Of course, it is not really going to be Jessica. It is some blooper of an American Idol audition that everyone laughs at with a horrible animal sound over it for good measure," I gushed out.

Mae's light bulb went off. She smiled. We smiled then, too, because we knew she had a plan.

As I changed out of my 'Jessica outfit' and put on clothes that made me feel more like me than I have in months, I smiled. Mae was talking a mile a minute about what we were going to do. Jordan was folding my 'Jessica outfit' and putting it in a bag to return later while inserting her opinions here and there. All feelings were getting back to normal. My heart was filling. I knew I had a lot of making up to do with them, but this was a start.

This was me coming home.

We ran out of my house just in time to catch the yellow school bus. I hadn't taken the bus with Mae and Jordan in so long that I stopped at its open door but couldn't climb up. Mae came up behind me and put her hand on my shoulder. She smiled, and I gained strength. I walked up the stairs and to our seats on the bus. This is what I was missing in the morning. Real connections with real friends, time to talk about each other, and about everything that had happened since we last talked. Due to our crazy circumstances this year, we couldn't catch up on everything on this bus ride, so we stuck to talking about what we needed to do as soon as we got off the bus.

I was going to have to avoid the car line. Charlotte and Raegan were riding together today and getting dropped off. I told them my mom was taking me so I could avoid them coming to my house to pick me up. Although that might have caused them to have some suspicion that something was wrong with me, I had no choice. They couldn't see that I was not wearing my 'Jessica outfit' before school.

As soon as the bus pulled over and its door opened, we all jumped out and jogged to the main doors. We raced into school and immediately spread out. We needed to find Jessica before Charlotte and Raegan got too far into their plan. We each took off down a different wing, looking for her. I tried to stay clear of the hallway with our lockers. The thought of facing Charlotte and Raegan in their outfits made me feel nauseous. I knew if they saw me in my jeans and not in my beige turtleneck, they would freak out. I need to focus on one thing at a time right now.

I quickly turned around the corner of a hallway, and I ran smack into Lucas. Literally.

"Ouch!" he laughed when he looked down and saw it was me.

"I'm so sorry! I am rushing and not watching where I am going."

"Where are you going in such a hurry? Your locker is in the other direction. I am just headed over there. Do you want to walk with me?" he asked. He stared at me while he waited for my answer. I hesitated but carefully responded.

"I'm not going to my locker right now." I put my head down. I was sure I was blushing a little. It probably showed that I was struggling with what to say next, too. I took a deep breath and spoke quickly. "I can't go there right now. I need to do something else, and Charlotte and Raegan can't see me yet. If I am being completely honest, I am looking for Jessica. I need to talk to her; it is important." I'm not sure why I just didn't tell him I had to go, but I stood there waiting for him to respond instead.

Lucas waited for me to say something else. When he realized I was done, he bent down to look me in the eye. "Does it have to do anything with what Charlotte and Raegan are wearing? I was wondering if you were going to show up in a similar outfit." I opened my mouth to respond but before I could respond, he added, "I am glad you didn't."

I looked up at him and smiled, a real smile. "Me too. I was supposed to, but I just couldn't do it. I had to finally stand up to them." He nodded a bit but stayed quiet, waiting for me to continue. "I need to find Jessica to make sure I can explain and help her through this morning and with the rest of the day. I just have to; it's the right thing to do." I knew I was talking fast because I was upset and had a lot to do. I needed to try to control my emotions, or else I wouldn't be good to anyone.

He nodded again and said, "I agree. I agree with everything you are saying. I am happy you feel this way. To be honest, I do too. I'll go and try to buy you some time. I'll tell the girls you are running late to school."

"I appreciate that. Thank you." I started to walk away, but I stopped and turned back around to look at him instead. "Lucas, why are you helping me? You know Charlotte and Raegan are going to be so mad at me, and maybe you, if I help Jessica. I'm pretty sure they are never going to speak to me again."

He smiled. "It is the right thing to do, LilyAnn. If you can do it, then so can I." Before I could respond, he was gone around the corner.

...

Jessica was sitting in the choir classroom by herself. Mae and I got there at the same time. I grabbed the doorknob and swung the door open. She was a bit startled by our entrance and jumped a bit in her seat where she sat with her head drooped in defeat. Tears were rolling down her face. It was obvious she saw the outfits and probably heard some comments already. It broke my heart to see her that upset, especially knowing that she didn't know this morning was only the beginning of Charlotte and Raegan's plan.

She wiped the tears from her cheeks and started to look questioningly at me and then at Mae. When Mae nodded at her and offered a slight smile, Jessica seemed to calm down any major concerns she might have had about me. When neither of us said anything, she just put her head back down on the desk in front of her.

We approached carefully, knowing that we had to be calm. We each sat down next to her. Mae put her hand on Jessica's shoulder.

"It's okay, Jessica. We are here for you. Both of us are here to help you," I said.

Jessica looked up at me with questions in her eyes. I smiled.

"I know you don't have any reason to trust me, and I understand your hesitation. But I am here to be helpful. To be kind to you."

She weakly smiled back. You could see she wanted to believe us, to have people on her side. I could tell by the expression on her face. Before I could think about it, I began talking. I told her how everything started, how I felt the whole time, where I was good to her, and where I wasn't. I told her all I knew about the plan for today. Everything from the outfits they were wearing, the signs and drama they were going to create, to the video they wanted to take and post on social media. Then I told her about the loudspeaker idea. She needed to know to be prepared in case we couldn't stop it. She needed to understand it all.

Unfortunately, we didn't have a lot of time for her to process it all before we needed to start strategizing if we were going to beat Charlotte at her own game.

# CHAPTER 18

# THE BYSTANDER IS A SQUARE PEG

I continued giving Jessica information. I was even telling her how I was struggling with the life I wanted to lead and the life I knew I should be living. I told her that no amount of popularity should come at the price of hurting people the way she was being hurt. Jessica's face began to soften, although her eyes still held so much pain. I told her I did not directly do anything to her, but I was there when the plans were being made and when people were saying mean things. I admitted I knew who the main source behind it all was. I told her I did nothing until now. I told her I was done being a bystander. There was no glory in being a bystander. I needed to be a square peg in this circle world we called middle school. I needed to be different and hoped others would appreciate it and maybe, just maybe, would also agree with me.

Jessica's tears seemed to turn from tears of sorrow to tears of appreciation. "You are willing to give up being in the most popular group in our grade, maybe even in our school, just to help me? Why?"

"I would. I am done watching things happen to people. I'm done watching things happen to you," I replied meekly.

"I can't even begin to tell you how much this means to me, LilyAnn, but I don't think I can get out of this chair and leave this room knowing what is happening out there right now," Jessica whispered.

Just then, Jordan came in and ran up to all of us. She went straight to Jessica and gave her a bear hug. Jessica laughed at this. It was the first time I had ever heard her laugh. That realization made me sad.

"Don't worry, Jessica. You don't have to. We've got you. You stay in here, and we'll be back."

With that, I got up and started to head out of the choir room with my head held high and Mae and Jordan right behind me. I knew the next place I needed to go. It was the place in school that had brought me happiness and laughter, as well as sadness and worry. It was the place that started to define me on day one of middle school. I turned the corner from the choir hallway and walked straight towards my locker by Charlotte's and Raegan's.

...

As I approached our locker section in the hallway, I heard the gasps people made when they saw me before I even saw Charlotte's and Raegan's expressions. It amazed me how everyone expected me to be a part of the plan. Now they were waiting for there to be a scene since I was in my jeans instead of the beige Jessica outfit.

Before I could finish my thought, Charlotte and Raegan both spun around and saw me. Both of their mouths dropped at the same time. I mean, their mouths were actually hanging wide open at the sight of me. Charlotte recovered first. She closed her mouth and adjusted herself, putting her hand on her hip and standing straighter than she was a second ago. Raegan quickly did the same. I just flashed a sweet smile and kept walking toward them until we were close enough to have a conversation without yelling down the hall.

"What are you wearing? Where is the outfit you are supposed to have on?" Charlotte hissed at me with anger in her voice. I had never heard her use that tone towards me before. I tried to stay calm and even out my breathing.

"This is exactly what I am supposed to be wearing. This is exactly what I am supposed to be doing." I smiled a bright smile at them both.

"What are you talking about? You are not making any sense!" Raegan spit back at me. I just kept smiling.

"I am feeling just fine. Better than I have in a while if I am being honest with myself." I took a brief pause to collect my nerves and then continued before I lost their attention. "I have been a witness, a bystander to what you both did and still plan to do to Jessica, for too long. When I asked you guys if it was right to do these things, you got mad at me. When I hesitated or left because I was sick to my stomach over some of your ideas, you never noticed or thought to ask me what was wrong."

Charlotte opened her mouth to say something, so I just put up my hand to stop her and continue.

"Don't get me wrong, that part was my fault. I am not blaming you for that. I should have spoken up earlier. I should have been louder when I did try. But I didn't, and I must live with that. However, I don't have to anymore. I can use my voice and tell you this is wrong, not just for

Jessica but for all the kids who get bullied every day, right here at Rose Middle. I will keep using my voice, and I will for as long as I need to. I have to stand up for people who are struggling to find the strength to do it for themselves."

I stopped talking. It sounded like everyone had stopped breathing. I swore you could hear a pin drop in the hallway. No one said a word. No one moved a muscle. I just stood there staring at Charlotte, waiting for her next move.

It came.

"Are you kidding me?" Charlotte hissed in my direction. Her voice was low and could hardly be heard. However, the venom could be easily detected. "You have to stand up for people? For her? Over being friends with us?"

Charlotte looked so mad. She also looked confused. No one had ever made the choice I was making at that moment.

I sighed. I knew in my heart it was going to come to this. I knew I'd have to choose. They wouldn't understand, or like that I went against them. My current reign at Rose Middle would have to end.

"I didn't want to choose between what is right or being friends with you, but if I have to, then yes. I pick standing up for people who need it."

Before anyone said anything else, I heard a noise and I saw Raegan fumbling in her locker. She looked like she was panicking, fumbling around in her locker. She yelled, "Ah Ha!" as she thrust her iPhone in the air. She started to look for something on it like her life depended on it.

Raegan screamed again, "Well, listen to the voice of the person you are trying to save!"

Charlotte went into defense mode and tried to grab the phone from her. There was a moment where all you could see were their four arms and long wavy hair intertwined. Charlotte made a final lunge for the phone but came up empty-handed.

She looked at Raegan and yelled at her, "Wait for the loudspeaker before you play that. There aren't enough people right now. You are ruining the next step in our plan, Raegan!"

Raegan laughed at Charlotte, which was a sound no one had ever heard before. She rolled her eyes and assured Charlotte it would be fine.

Before Charlotte could object again, Raegan hit play. A horrible sound came out of the speaker and floated through the hallway. Someone was singing. Everyone stopped talking at once to listen, to try to make it all out. The voice was terrible. It was off-key and sounded like it was screaming at times. Raegan stood there with the phone in the air while people just stared at her. For the first time, Charlotte did not seem to know what to do next. Only a few people were whispering right now. If I was going to do anything, I had to make my move.

I giggled loudly.

Charlotte and Raegan both swung their heads in my direction, their eyes throwing daggers at me.

"That is not a real recording of Jessica. It doesn't even remotely sound like her actual voice. You can pretend all you want, but you know the truth. You both have heard her sing. I was with you. That is why you developed the video idea, right? There is no way you two wanted anyone to hear her voice because it is beautiful. Magical, really."

Charlotte and Raegan stood there, not saying a word to me, to anyone. Their eyes were piercing through me. Any whispering there was in the hallway had completely stopped. All eyes were on me.

I noticed Lucas was making his way to the front of the group. The way he was looking at me, reassured me at that moment. Everyone was waiting to hear what I would say next, but right then, the bell rang. At first, no one moved. Then people slowly started making their way to class. As they walked away in different directions, they all turned around at least once to see if they were missing anything.

They weren't.

I finally stopped shaking.

# CHAPTER 19

# BYSTANDERS CAN'T DO IT ALONE

As the hallways started to thin out, everyone was still talking at once. I made sure to leave with the crowd, to blend in as I left. I was not ready to face Charlotte and Raegan just yet. That would come later. Mae and Jordan started walking with the crowd too. They made sure to stay right behind me as we tried to find a space to be alone for a second. We walked to an empty corridor. I turned around to see them beaming at me. They both looked around to make sure we were alone and then they started squealing with delight and giving me hugs.

"We are so proud of you!" Jordan gushed as she put her arms around my shoulder.

I wanted to thank them right away, but I blushed instead. It felt bad to be getting praise for doing something I should have done so much earlier, or never should have been a part of to begin with. However, I would take the win for now. I'd be proud of the fact that I turned down popularity to do the right thing.

"Thank you guys, for everything. For answering my call this morning. For coming over so quickly to help me and for helping me remember who I am."

There were more hugs and even a few tears. When we settled down, I continued, "I do think I have to go to the principal's office and let him know what has been going on. It amazes me that it has gotten this far. He needs to know so he can deal with it... and so that I can ask about my second part of the plan."

Mae jumped up and down. "Really? Really? Are you going to ask him?"

"If Jessica is still up for it, then of course! It will blow people's minds. We need to help her do something. Although Jessica is only one person, I am sure there are others that people are making fun of that we don't know about. We must start making a change. We need to send a message," I said passionately.

Mae and Jordan looked at each other and then at me.

"We agree," they said at the same time and then hugged me again.

...

Instead of going to the first period, I went straight to the principal's office. He was happy to fit me in when I explained to the secretary why I was there. As I sat and waited for him to call me in his office, I had time to think about how this scenario might play out. Was there a possibility that I could get in trouble? I believed there was. Was there a chance he would not let me do the second part of our plan? I believed there was a chance of that too. I needed to make sure that he understood how strongly I felt about making a change in the school. I may have been a small part of the problem, but I really wanted to be a big part of the change too. I wanted to make a difference here.

A few minutes later, he came out to get me from the chair I was starting to sink into. I followed him to his office and he shut the door. Here we go.

He showed me to some chairs, and I sat down in the one that looked the most uncomfortable. I needed to be on my game and pay attention to what I was saying and how I was saying it. That required me to sit in a straight wooden chair instead of the super soft-looking leather one. I sat and waited for him to pick a chair and sit as well. Once he was all ready for me to begin, I started spilling everything, probably too much. I went into detail about how I wanted to be popular, fit in, and be accepted. I explained how we all started to talk over the summer and the distress I was often under because of how hard it was being their friend.

I went on and on.

He sat patiently and listened to me the whole time I talked. I started getting into the more recent events.

I told him about what had been happening in school, how Jessica was getting made fun of everywhere she went by several people now. It was no longer just Charlotte and Raegan. I told him about the locker room and the sign. I told him about the social media videos. I told him how her demeanor had changed since she first got there. That was the hardest to explain. As I did, my hands shook some, and I got teary-eyed. He got up just long enough to hand me a box of tissues. I took one, dried my eyes, and kept going. I explained why the videos were posted and about the plan for that day. I told him about the outfit I was going to wear today but just couldn't.

Finally, I explained what happened this morning at school. I started with how we got to school and looked for Jessica right away. I told him how defeated she looked when we found her in the choir room, how she didn't even want to leave that classroom. I told him that I left her there since she felt safe and tried to put an end to her misery. That was when I told him about my confrontation with Charlotte and Raegan.

I explained everything. I described every emotion I felt, from scared to brave to worried to relieved. I told him what they were wearing and why. I told him how all the kids were by Charlotte and Raegan in the hall and how I got reprimanded for not doing what I was supposed to, reprimanded for not being mean. I let him know everything I said to them and everything they said back to me. I finally explained how Raegan took out the phone and played a voice, telling everyone it was Jessica's. I also went into detail about why that was a significant moment. I told him about the loudspeaker plan. I told him I had no idea how they were going to get on the loudspeaker, though. I was not there for that part of the plan. I just thought I should mention that since I was already on a roll.

After I finished telling him about walking out of the hallway with Mae and Jordan to avoid Charlotte and Raegan, I stopped talking. I finally took a deep breath. He was quietly looking at me. I saw different emotions cross his face. I couldn't figure out what was going on in his head.

He got up from behind his desk and came to sit next to me. "Thank you, LilyAnn, for sharing this story. Your story. Jessica's story."

I nodded at him, not able to find words.

"First, let me apologize. You are right. An adult should have intervened long before it got this far, long before you had to do all of this. I am embarrassed and sad that people have missed signs, that I have missed the signs. And if what you are saying is accurate, which I believe it is, many people missed actual, physical signs. For that, and for so much more, I apologize."

I started crying. I was ugly crying. I didn't even know where all the tears were coming from, but the gate was open, and relief flooded out of me.

He waited for me to calm down and then handed me the box of tissues again. As I took them, his look reassured me, so I started to calm down.

"Please know that I will apologize to Jessica today. I will also be contacting her family to inform them of what has been going on and to apologize as well. Furthermore, I will be talking to all the teachers about everything you have said. We have some work to do here at Rose Middle School to ensure each and every student feels safe coming into our school."

I smiled at him and thanked him for listening to me, for believing me, and for helping Jessica. He started to get up from his chair but sat back down quickly.

"Before I let you go, is there anything else I can do for you right now?"

Actually, boy was there!

"I am so glad you asked. I wasn't sure how to bring up the fact that I needed a favor. But I do."

He smiled at me and gestured for me to go on. I then explained my idea, my second part to confronting Charlotte and Raegan that morning. The idea included Jessica having a lot of trust in me and, more importantly, herself. Again, as I talked and explained all the details, he just listened. When I was done, I stopped fidgeting with my hands and looked up at him, waiting to hear his thoughts.

"I will say your plan is unconventional. It is not the way we would normally do things after a conversation like the one we just had. However, I do like the idea of it being student-driven, giving students a voice. I do want to take a stand against any bullying that is going on in the school." He paused and looked like he was deep in thought. "So, I am going to allow you to go forward with your plan. Since both you and Jessica have PE last period. Come to the office then. We'll do it at the end of the day, so there is little academic time interrupted, but the point will still be made. Does this work for you, Miss. LilyAnn?"

Although I was super nervous, I was smiling from ear to ear. I nodded vigorously as I responded, "It does. Thank you so much."

As I stood up, he stopped me. "No, thank you so much. I know doing what you just did is not easy. I also know you are not 100% innocent in what happened, yet here you are, explaining the whole story. You are being brave, kind, and thoughtful. You are putting someone else's happiness before your own, and that is exactly how I would have liked to see you grow from this situation. This is a life lesson you are learning. It is the best outcome I could hope for you. However, I want you to know I will be calling home for you too. I will be telling your parents what happened, but in the end, learning that lesson and doing what you are doing today will be the only consequence you get from me."

I was so relieved I jumped up and hugged him.

"Thank you. I appreciate that. I have learned, really."

He laughed. "I believe you have. LilyAnn, I am so proud of you. I will be telling your parents that as well. You did something amazing today. You are not a bystander anymore."

"Thank you, sir." I was smiling because I was happy and tearing up. After all, let's be honest, it had been an emotional day.

The crazy part was that the day wasn't over yet.

Not even close.

## CHAPTER 20

## A DAY FULL OF SURPRISES

As I walked out of the principal's office, I saw Mae, Jordan, and Jessica sitting in the front office waiting for me. I couldn't smile any bigger.

"What are you guys doing here?"

Jessica broke the silence first. "I couldn't have you doing all my fighting for me." She looked up and smiled. "I am ready to talk too, to stand up for myself, because of you. Thank you."

I ran up to her and hugged her fiercely.

"He said yes. He is going to help us with our plan. We will go over the details before PE, but get your singing voice ready, friend. The whole school is going to hear that beautiful voice of yours today! And yes, I mean the whole school. We don't have to wait until the musical auditions." I joked.

Jessica smiled. It felt so good to see her do that. She gave me one more hug and whispered that she was in and that she would be ready. Just then, the principal opened his office door and called Jessica back to his office. Mae, Jordan, and I opened the office door and walked out arm in arm.

It felt funny trying to avoid the people I had idolized for so long. I found myself walking down hallways I hadn't walked down all year. I was actively trying to avoid Charlotte and Raegan instead of trying to get their attention. It was a weird turn of events. As I was on my way to math, a different way of course, I turned a corner and walked right into Lucas and JR. Both their eyes flew right to mine. I wasn't sure why I was nervous, but I was. I sucked in my breath and held it.

"You and corners, LilyAnn, you are dangerous. You're going to hurt someone one day with your use of them," Lucas said at the same time as he was laughing.

I couldn't help it. I let out my breath and laughed out loud. "Sorry, I am all over the place today. I have a lot on my mind."

"I bet you do," JR said under his breath with something in his voice I couldn't quite figure out yet.

Was he mad at me? Was he confused by what I did? Was he scared to talk to me because Charlotte would get mad at him? I had no idea.

"JR," Lucas whispered as he shot him a look that said, 'Hey man, chill.'

"It's fine," I said confidently. "I know I am not everyone's favorite person right now. Especially if you are good friends with Charlotte and Raegan. But I do know I finally did the right thing. Being mean isn't the only option to people who aren't like us or to people who threaten us in some way. I am hoping one day more people will agree with me and with what I did."

JR was quiet for a minute but then said, "Yeah, I guess." I called it a victory, so I smiled and started to walk toward math class.

As soon as I took a step, Lucas grabbed my arm. I turned around and looked at him. He smiled and gave me a thumbs-up before he turned and walked away with JR.

That one gesture made me feel so much better than I had just a moment ago. No matter what happened next, I knew I was doing good. People were either going to be behind me or not. When I stopped to think about it, even the ones who might not be behind me probably knew they should be.

...

I quickly ran to my locker during class to grab a folder I had forgotten. I was trying to hustle when I swung the locker door open. As soon as it opened, I jumped back. Notes fell from inside my locker to the floor. Notes were everywhere. Some were just small pieces of paper with messages on them, some were whole pieces of paper that were folded up, some were Post-Its with a few words or emojis, and some were even on construction paper. I quickly glanced at what they said. They all looked like positive messages to me for either standing up for Jessica, standing up to Charlotte and Raegan, or just standing up for someone who needed help in general.

As soon as I realized what these notes meant, my heart burst with happiness and pride for what I was doing. It made me so glad to know that all these people not only believed in what I was doing, but they had made an effort to find time this morning to write me a note just to let me know. I was beyond grateful for these gifts of encouragement.

I fell to my knees and started picking up the papers. As I did, tears started rolling down my face again. I was not sure where this unexpected emotion was coming from, but it was wrapping around my heart. It was so strong and full of importance I could hardly breathe.

After taking a minute to let myself enjoy this moment, it hit me. I was relieved this morning for standing up to the girls and what I believed in, but at this moment, I felt sad. I was sad that so many people couldn't do what I did this morning. I was sad that so many people felt there was a need for this kind of action. The proof was right here on the floor in front of me. I didn't want people to feel alone in this fight. I knew right then my part in all of this was going to have to go far beyond my stunt today.

# CHAPTER 21

# LOUDSPEAKER

All during PE, Jessica and I went over what we were going to do when the time came to go to the office and get on the loudspeaker. I might have even been more nervous than she was. Okay, that wasn't true. I knew she was crazy nervous. With 15 minutes left in the period, we handed our passes to the PE teacher and headed to the office. When we got there, we reviewed what we were going to say one last time and then headed over to the loudspeaker. We walked over there with our shoulders pushed back, our heads held high, and nervous smiles on our faces. We were as ready as we'd ever be. We stared at the microphone and the big, red button on the loudspeaker for a long second. We knew that when we hit that button, what we were going to do and say would be heard by everyone in the whole school. Everyone. There was no going back. We needed to make sure we were all in. We made eye contact and smiled. I grabbed her hand and gave it a squeeze for reassurance.

We were all in.

The principal looked over at us and waited until I let go of Jessica's hand and turned towards him. He was trying to look impartial, but his grin was showing just enough for us to know he was behind us. He nodded at us and hit the button on the loudspeaker. The crackling-sounding noise could be heard throughout the whole school. The principal cleared his throat and began.

"Excuse this interruption, ladies and gentlemen. We have a short announcement that needs your attention this afternoon. I will now hand over the microphone to LilyAnn and Jessica."

Breathe. Breathe. Breathe.

"Good afternoon, everyone. My name is LilyAnn. William Shakespeare said, 'It is not in the stars to hold our destiny but in ourselves.' I have come to learn that this quote has multiple meanings. To start, we each need to be in charge of our own destiny and our paths to get there. I have learned that this year. I am hoping to help others learn that for themselves as well. I'll let you know more about that tomorrow. For now, I'd like to help someone find their destiny today. I want to introduce you to a star we have right here in Rose Middle. Mr. Hamill was keeping her a secret until the spring musical, but I feel we could all use a little star power this afternoon. I'd like Rose Middle to hear the real Jessica."

I handed the microphone over to Jessica. As she took it, she softly closed her eyes. I turned my head away from her just in time to see Charlotte and Raegan coming down the hall towards the office window. The looks on their faces were amazing, borderline perfect. They were a mixture of disbelief, anger, and horror. I couldn't tell if the disbelief was in my strength to go against them or that we had hijacked their loudspeaker idea. Either way, Charlotte was glaring at us, clearly shaking with rage – that much was clear.

Jessica didn't even notice them. She hovered her hand over the button and looked at me. I covered her hand with mine reassuringly.

I whispered, "You got this. You are a star." Then I hit the button.

She moved the microphone closer to her and she began to speak.

"Hey, Tigers. My name is Jessica. I'm going to sing a quick song for you."

And sing she did. Her angelic voice carried across the loudspeakers, through each hallway, in each classroom, to each student in the school. It was amazing. People who didn't know her before definitely did now. Kids who had made fun of her voice would never do so again. Those who teased her for what she wore or for her hair would see past all that and only remember this moment going forward. This moment was magic. I was so proud of her, of us.

Mae and Jordan ran down the hall, past Charlotte and Raegan who were storming away from the office, and right into my outstretched arms as Jessica sang. We hugged and then swayed together as Jessica kept singing, sounding more beautiful as her confidence grew.

"You guys are amazing!" Jordan whispered to me. "I do have a question, though, what is the big plan you are sharing with the whole school tomorrow?"

I laughed. "I am not sure. I have a few ideas I am tossing around in my head. I officially have tonight to work them all out and to turn whichever the best idea is into reality, I guess." I shrugged my shoulders, feeling doubtful for the first time in hours.

"Don't worry," Mae softly said to both of us. "You have us to help you tonight."

Just then, Jessica stopped singing and put down the loudspeaker. She ran over and hugged us all. We all started talking at once. We knew this was a special moment and couldn't wait to get home to make it even better.

## CHAPTER 22

## OUR NEXT MOVE

We all got on the bus. That big, stinky, yellow bus that I had tried to avoid all year. I did not avoid it today; I was excited about it. To be honest, I forgot how fun this part was, all of us together talking, discussing our day, connecting. I had never been so happy to ride a school bus home. As the four of us were talking, some of the kids around us turned in our direction. They started to chime into our conversation. They said something nice or even funny to Mae, Jordan, or me. Most importantly, though, they complimented Jessica. They told her she was brave or how good they thought her voice was. It was the coolest ride home.

The bus stopped on our street, and we all rushed down the aisle and out the door. We could barely talk. We were running so quickly. I opened the front door, we all ran in, yelled hello to my mom, and then proceeded upstairs to my room. Jordan was the last one in. She shut the bedroom door behind her. Mae stepped around me and opened my closet door.

"We need to add another lesson, don't you think?"

"Yes, yes I do," I smiled.

I went to my dresser and grabbed a Sharpie. I walked to the closet with the Sharpie in the air like a trophy. As I walked past Jessica, I saw that she looked confused. I laughed out loud.

"Oh, my goodness, this must look and sound ridiculous if you don't know the story behind it. Okay, girls, where do we begin?"

They both immediately yelled, "The beginning!"

So, I did.

...

After a lot of talking and trips down memory lane, I headed back towards the closet door. I took off the cap and wrote down the number nine under my last lesson.

"So, what will it be? What are we writing for number 9?"

It was a debate for a while; we all had such good ideas. After going back and forth, we came up with the perfect lesson.

I wrote it down.

LESSONS LEARNED

1. NEVER PUT A SQUARE PEG IN A ROUND HOLE

2. ALWAYS BE KIND

3. ALWAYS TELL THE TRUTH (you'll get in less trouble)

4. DON'T FORGET TO HAVE GOOD SPORTSMANSHIP

5. TRY TO SEE THE BEST IN OTHERS

6. BE KIND: NO BULLYING

7. SCHOOL IS HARD, FAMILY IS HARD, & SOMETIMES FRIENDSHIPS ARE THE HARDEST

8. ALWAYS REMEMBER TO BE A SQUARE PEG IN A WORLD OF ROUND HOLES

9. IT IS NOT IN THE STARS TO HOLD OUR DESTINY BUT IN OURSELVES

"Alright, ladies. That is awesome. Now we just have to decide what our destiny is. What is the name we want to make for ourselves? What is the future we want to see? Most importantly, what is the legacy we want to leave behind?"

I asked everyone these tough questions because I needed help answering them for myself. I was hoping we could figure it all out together.

Everyone started throwing around words like change, positivity, making a difference, friendships, and inspiration. With all our talking and passion, an idea was born.

We all got on our social media apps and got to work. We needed to do some research. We needed to see what other schools were doing already, what was working and what wasn't working. We needed to compare it to our idea to make sure we were on the right path. We saw some similar ideas and investigated how they got them started. In the end, our idea felt like it was the right amount of our voices, and our passion, yet still had the logistics to be successful.

Tomorrow morning there was going to be a different presence at Rose Middle, and it was going to change some worlds. At least we hoped.

...

I got up the next day with a different spring in my step. It's funny – I woke up yesterday ready to get dressed up for school to complete a plan. Today I was doing it again, except it was so different. Yesterday I was hesitant, nauseous, nervous, and even sad. Today I was excited, passionate, determined and, best of all, happy.

As I was getting ready for school, my mom knocked on the door.

"Come in!" I was standing there, ready to go to school, ready to make some positive noise.

My mom opened her mouth to say something, then shut it. Her smile was ear to ear. She didn't have to say anything; I knew what she was thinking. She walked right over to me and gave me a bear hug.

"This is so much more like it. This is a perfect example of the beauty and strength I have always known you possess. I am so proud of you."

I wiped a tear from my eye. As I did, I noticed she was doing the same. It felt good to start doing positive work and have it be noticed at home. When my mom was proud of me, I knew I was doing the world some good.

We walked out of my room, ready to start the day. My mom offered to drive me to school, but I declined. That day was a 'take the yellow school bus to school' kind of day!

...

When the four of us got just outside of school, we stopped walking and stood in a group. We needed to take out our secret weapons for the day and put them on.

We put the sandwich boards over our heads and into place, then started to walk through the main doors together. We were walking arm in arm as we went in. We immediately received some big, positive feedback. I mean, we *were* essentially wearing big posters. Two of the boards had our new Instagram account on them, and the other two had the new Snapchat account we all created. Both the accounts had the name, 'Rose Middle Positivity' on them in big, bold letters.

As we took a few more steps inside, kids started coming up to us, asking us all about the posters. We all had the same practiced response. It even made people laugh a little when we said it at the same time. There was so much good happening in this moment that I almost forgot I would have to face Charlotte and Raegan.

I remembered as soon as I saw them barreling down the hallway, straight toward me. I braced myself and got ready to use our practiced stock response.

"What are these sandwich boards all about, LilyAnn? Take them off! This has gone far enough!" Charlotte demanded.

"I am so glad you asked what these posters are all about! These posters show the new social media presence we have started for Rose Middle School. We have started a way to help spread positivity throughout the school. Everyone will be able to read what positive things people are saying about others, and it is all anonymous, so there is no glory in saying anything, just positive vibes when reading them. We want people to post thoughts, pictures, questions, and anything they want in a safe, supportive place. It will be full of compliments, shout-outs, and fun. We are working on making this school a place students want to be, not fear to be. Would you like to write something positive?" I asked with the biggest smile on my face.

"Ugh. As if!" Raegan cried.

"I don't even understand why you are doing this. No one was saying mean things about you. You were hanging out with us. Your life was great. Why are you trying so hard to help others feel good about themselves? Why couldn't you just leave things the way they were?" Charlotte sounded like she was whining as she asked the questions.

"My life may have seemed great, but I was missing something. You guys were fun and popular, and I loved it. I do appreciate how you included me. Really, I do. But I wasn't fully satisfied. I was missing my friends who kept me grounded, and most of all, I was missing my strength, and my ability to help others, not make them feel awful. I worry about kids who don't want to come to school every day because they struggle, because they feel invisible, or worse because peers are making fun of them," I explained to them. I realized when I said it just how true it was.

"If I knew you would have turned out like this, I would have never brought you into our inner circle. You care too much about people outside our friend group. Worst of all, the way you are acting is making people think I'm horrible for the things I have done."

"Don't you think they are horrible things?" I asked her honestly.

Charlotte paused and looked thoughtful for a second. Before I could wonder if she was contemplating what I asked, she snapped back to herself.

"Whatever. Your efforts are so pointless. No one is ever going to post on your accounts. No one is going to care about being positive. People like it when I make fun of people. They laugh. People are going to start to laugh at you too. Just saying," she snorted. Just then, a group of 8th graders walked down the hallway. They took out their phones and snapped the QR code. "Ha. See LilyAnn, I told you. Now the 8th graders are going to make fun of you. This is going to be awesome!"

The 8th grade girl, Payton, who was wearing a cheerleading uniform, gave Charlotte a dirty look. "We are not here to make fun of her. Anyone who would say that doesn't know what they are talking about or what is cool."

Kids were flocking into the hallway around us as she talked to Charlotte. Charlotte's face was flaming red from anger and embarrassment.

"We came down here to tell LilyAnn how incredible we think this idea is. We are a little jealous that a 6th grader thought of it before one of us," Payton laughed. "It is brilliant and just what this school needs! It's going to be such fun."

"Thank you!" I heard Jessica respond before I could even say a word.

Payton looked at her. "That voice. Are you the one that sang over the loudspeaker?"

Jessica nodded.

"Amazing!" Payton exclaimed. "Can I have the sign you are wearing to put up in the $8^{th}$ grade hallway? I want to make sure everyone sees what you guys have started. I'll have it added to the morning announcements as well."

Jessica gave her the poster she was wearing and thanked her for her compliments. As she started to walk away, Payton whispered something to me that I would take with me forever. That was the last thing Charlotte and Raegan needed to see. They both stormed away down the hall. As I watched them walk away, I chuckled, but only a little bit. It had been a fantastic morning.

...

As I was appreciating all the things that had happened so far that morning, Lucas came up behind me and put his elbow on my shoulder.

I looked up at him while he said, "Good morning! You know you are making a huge difference here today, don't you, LilyAnn?" I smiled at him, and he continued. "You are quite amazing. It is not every day that someone will take the chance of giving up their popularity to do what is right for others. Then in the process, do amazing things for the school. You are a hero. The best part is, although I know it is hard to imagine, you might just end up more popular than when you were hanging out with Charlotte."

"Oh, stop it," I said as I blushed.

"I can't, it's true. You have already got a lot of people thinking in different ways, and it is pretty cool. Even JR doesn't know if he should text Charlotte or get on your new page right now," Lucas said as he laughed.

I laughed as well. I loved it.

Just then, Mae, Jordan, and Jessica came over to us.

"I can't believe this morning turned out the way it did," Jordan sing-songed. "Let's make sure we hand out the information to anyone who shows any interest all day long. I want these sights to blow up by this afternoon."

We all saluted her and headed off to class. For the first time in a long time, I didn't want to avoid any of my classes.

...

Two days later, Mae, Jordan, Jessica, Lucas, JR, and I were sitting in the cafeteria at our new table. It was the longest table that included anyone who wanted to sit there. Depending on the day, there were kids who love academics, kids who loved sports, kids who loved the arts, and even kids who were super quiet. We loved that at our table at lunch, everyone was equal.

We were on our social media apps, looking at what had been posted in the last two days. It was crazy! There was so much to look at, read, and admire.

Students had posted pictures of friends with sweet comments. There were pictures of student artwork with fun, supportive emojis attached. Kids had posted their positive thoughts or shout-outs to people. Every time I saw a new picture or read a comment, I smiled.

My heart was full.

## CHAPTER 23

# A FEW MONTHS LATER – SPRING MUSICAL DAY

I woke up on the morning of the spring musical and grabbed my phone. I started each morning by looking at my favorite page on both Instagram and Snapchat. This had become my ritual since we'd created the pages. It brought me such joy to wake up and see positive things being said about different people on so many different platforms every day. I never realized our idea would have such an effect on people.

When we began this journey, I wanted to make a difference in Jessica's life. I never imagined we could make a difference for others, too. After my daily dose of happiness, I got out of bed and hopped over to my dresser to grab my Sharpie. I knew in my bones it was time for another life lesson: Number 10!

LESSONS LEARNED

1. NEVER PUT A SQUARE PEG IN A ROUND HOLE

2. ALWAYS BE KIND

3. ALWAYS TELL THE TRUTH (you'll get in less trouble)

4. DON'T FORGET TO HAVE GOOD SPORTSMANSHIP

5. TRY TO SEE THE BEST IN OTHERS

6. BE KIND: NO BULLYING

7. SCHOOL IS HARD, FAMILY IS HARD, & SOMETIMES FRIENDSHIPS ARE THE HARDEST

8. ALWAYS REMEMBER TO BE A SQUARE PEG IN A WORLD OF ROUND HOLES

9. IT IS NOT IN THE STARS TO HOLD OUR DESTINY BUT IN OURSELVES

10. IF YOU CAN MAKE A DIFFERENCE, ALWAYS MAKE A DIFFERENCE

I laid my Sharpie down and stared at my newest addition. I fully believed in number 10 and hoped to spend a good part of my life devoted to trying to make it a reality. I stood there and thought for just a few minutes before I snapped back to the here and now. I needed to get going. I started moving at a faster pace, got dressed, and put my hair up. There was a lot to do today, and I was so ready for it.

I needed to pick up my outfit for the musical tonight and make sure the theater department was all set to go. I needed to run to the flower shop to get a bouquet for Jessica. I had ordered a beautiful arrangement with school-colored ribbons on it. I wanted her to know how much she was appreciated at Rose Middle. I also wanted her to know how proud I was of her for getting the lead. Not that anyone doubted she would after she sang to the school for what will go down as the coolest singing moment in Rose's history! I was so blessed to be a part of that moment.

I had thought a lot about that moment during the last few months. I often went back to it in my mind and broke down what happened. It's a little embarrassing to admit, but I had amazed myself. Not that I had done anything crazy amazing, but I tried to appreciate that I had the nerve to stand up to Charlotte and Raegan. So many people's lives got better after that day. What I did mattered. It mattered in ways I didn't expect it to. I felt that was a truly defining day for me – a day I saw what I could do and what I could change if I put my mind to it.

Whenever I doubt myself, or my place in this crazy life, I think of that and remember what I can do. I remember what I already did.

...

I was trying to quickly run errands downtown, hoping to get back to the house in good time. I walked out of the flower shop and made a quick right as the door closed. I walked smack into someone again. Of course, I literally ran into Lucas. I gasped and put my hand to my mouth. I started to apologize, but before I could say anything, Lucas put his hand in the air to stop me and started to laugh.

"I know, I know. You weren't paying attention. You were in a rush and didn't see me."

"Exactly! I am sorry. It is crazy how I keep doing that to you."

"It is okay; it's become a habit I look forward to," Lucas responded, and I blushed. "I am kind of glad we ran into each other. I have been thinking about something for a few days now and was trying to find the right time to talk to you."

A light shade of red slowly crept up his face when he was done with that confession. I couldn't tell if he wanted me to respond or wait for him to continue. I decided to wait.

"I think you have done so many incredible things this year. When I look back on all the wonderful, thoughtful, brave things you have done, I am so proud of you. I wanted to find a good time to tell you that. Most importantly, I am grateful that even when you were struggling with everything that was going on, we were always good. When things exploded, we were good. It's just nice to know that no matter what happens, we will always be there for each other."

When he finished, he fidgeted with his hands in his pockets and rocked back and forth.

I smiled. I smiled a deep, authentic, and warm smile.

"I am so grateful for that as well. I am so grateful for you," I said a little sheepishly. As I said the words, I realized how deeply I meant them. I reached out for his hands that he had just taken out of his pocket. I took both of his hands and squeezed them.

Before I could say anything else, he leaned forward and hugged me. The hug said so much, but at that moment, I was just grateful for it. I didn't overthink it. I leaned in and hugged him tight. We stayed like that for a minute, and then we separated. The red in his cheeks grew a shade deeper as we made eye contact.

"I better get going," I said just loud enough for him to hear.

"OK. I'll see you there tonight. Make sure you save me a seat next to you," he responded. I nodded my head, grinned, and then started to walk away.

I stopped.

Before I could overthink it, I turned back and kissed his cheek – then I turned to leave again. Before I took another step, I took a quick look at his face. He was smiling. All was good. I walked down the street, trying not to run into anyone else, grinning like a fool.

...

After I got home, I called Mae and Jordan to tell them to come over. We were getting ready at my house where it all started. Minutes later they were at my bedroom door. I ran to unlock it and threw my arms around them.

"Happy Musical Day!" I screamed at them while laughing.

They laughed too, and we started getting ready. We blared our music, danced around the room, and laughed a lot. When we were good and out of breath, we decided to get dressed. I took a few extra minutes to make sure my hair looked perfect and added my favorite lip gloss. I smiled at my reflection and faced the girls.

We were ready.

I opened my mouth to tell them what happened with Lucas, but I quickly shut it. I was going to hang on to that just for me for a little while.

...

We walked downstairs, and my mom caught us before we left to take a quick picture. As she grabbed her phone to take the shot, she hesitated. I saw her wipe her eyes again.

"What's wrong, mom?" I asked her, looking concerned. She just shook her head and wiped her cheeks.

"Nothing is wrong. It is the exact opposite of wrong. I am so proud of you girls. So extremely proud of the young women you have all become. My heart is full," she told us. We all ran to her and gave her a bear hug. Now we were ready to leave.

...

We walked into the auditorium arm in arm. We took a second to admire the room, to reflect on how far we had come to get to this point. I looked at each of my best friends, the sweetest, strongest girls I could have by my side and smiled at them.

We made our way over to our seats.

A few minutes later, Lucas and JR joined us. Lucas sat next to me in the seat I promised to save for him. JR didn't even flinch as Lucas sat next to me – he just went to the end of the four of us and sat next to Mae. They immediately started chatting.

With only a few minutes before the musical started, a woman I had never met stopped at the end of our row. She paused and made eye contact with me.

"Are you LilyAnn?" Before I could ask her who she was, she followed up with, "I don't mean to catch you off guard, I just wanted to meet you. I am Jessica's mom. She told me where you would be sitting."

"Yes, ma'am. I am LilyAnn. It is so nice to meet you. This is Mae and Jordan. They are Jessica's friends too," I shared. "And the boys, Lucas and JR, are huge Jessica supporters as well," I beamed as I said this to her.

"Hello, everyone. It is my absolute pleasure to meet each of you," she admitted as her eyes got a little glassy. "LilyAnn, I wanted to catch you to give you a little something I made for you. I've been meaning to drop it off at your house before tonight but haven't found the time. I'm a single mom who works two jobs, so I haven't had much free time to get it to you."

"Oh, you are too sweet. You didn't have to do anything for me."

"I didn't have to, but I really wanted to. It's not a big deal or anything, but what you did is a big deal. You gave my daughter a new life. Not just at this school, but overall. She has confidence and joy in her now. I haven't seen anything like it since she was a young girl. Between you sticking up for her to the wonderful positivity page you all have started, she smiles. She also sings again. There is absolutely no price tag on that," Jessica's mom shared as she handed me a small box.

I pulled apart the beautiful bow and opened it. Inside was a gorgeously detailed, hand carved angel.

"Oh, my goodness. It is beautiful. I can't believe you made this."

"You are so welcome. I was happy too. I picked an angel for a specific reason. You are Jessica's guardian angel. Please remember that."

"Thank you so much," was all I could whisper.

Jessica's mom whispered another, "You're welcome." Before she moved to her seat, she hesitated before asking, "Can I give you a hug?"

I immediately jumped up, leaned over Lucas, and hugged Jessica's mom. She hugged me with such appreciation and love. I would always remember that moment when I needed strength to help someone else be strong. She gave me one last, beaming smile, and then she walked to her seat in the front row.

I was still a bit emotional as the lights dimmed, giving us all a 3-minute warning before the musical began. I couldn't help smiling. I looked around the auditorium in awe. What an experience middle school had been already. So many great things had happened, so many bright spots when – at times – I wasn't sure if there would be any. As the lights dimmed for the last time, the musical started. Lucas grabbed my hand and gave it a little squeeze.

Jessica took the stage with two 8th graders in an opening number that brought the house down. People were clapping and whistling before the song was even over. It went on like this throughout the whole show. The auditorium was full of an electricity that was hard to explain but so easy to feel.

The show ended, and everyone erupted with cheers and clapping. Every single person in the auditorium was on their feet. Some people even started to chant Jessica's name in admiration of her performance. Mae, Jordan and I were the loudest. Jessica came back on for her final bow of the performance. I walked up to the stage and presented her with the flower bouquet I had picked up that morning. She was so full of emotions as she took them and hugged me. She was smiling bigger than I had ever seen, but she also looked so appreciative.

"Thank you for believing in me, LilyAnn," is all I heard her say as I moved away so she could have the spotlight.

...

As the auditorium started to clear out, we all jumped on the stage and sat on the edge while we waited for Jessica to get changed. At that moment, I was so completely happy. I was reveling in the feeling, thinking there was no way I could feel happier than I did at that moment.

That was when I got a notification on my phone. It was from the Rose Middle Positivity page. I opened it and read it:

> *Thank you to a special group of people. To LilyAnn and everyone who sat with her tonight during the musical. To Jessica, that killed every song she sang tonight. Thank you for making me reflect and re-evaluate how I treat people, what I value and what I think real friendship is. Maybe one day you will all forgive me. Maybe one day we can all be friends*

*again. Until then, I will post something positive every day. Love Charlotte.*

I turned off my phone, held it to my chest and closed my eyes. I felt so complete and blessed at this moment. I opened my eyes and looked at all my friends on the stage.

I smiled with the realization that we were all going to get through middle school and, with any luck, high school too.

We would get through it all as friends, as leaders, and as people who continued to inspire change and positivity.

Be a square peg.

# READING COMPREHENSION QUESTION TYPES

***Factual:*** explicit questions, black and white questions, focus on obvious details that are in the text. First, identify the details. Second, remove irrelevant parts of the text.

> Examples: Who, What, Where, When, Why and How questions. What did the character do after school? Why did the character cry?

***Inferencing:*** implicit questions, harder than factual questions, need to understand a "hidden" or concealed meaning that is suggested. The information is not directly said or shared with the reader.

> Examples: She jumped up and down, smiling. (you can infer she is happy). Why was the character sad? How do you know that to be true?

***Sequencing:*** requires statement of the events in order. In the text; what happened first, it does not matter which event appears first in the text. It is literally which event was first, second, and so on.

> Examples: What happened first, second, third, and last? What were the 5 main events of the passage, in order? What three happen after the character closes the door?

**Predicting:** use of 'clues' from the text combined with personal knowledge and experiences to anticipate what might happen next. The more that is read, the more information is gathered (then able to revise predictions)

> Examples: What does the title tell us about what the book will be about? What do you think will happen next?

**Making Connections:** deals with activating prior knowledge, focus on teaching to make connections between a text and their own experiences and understanding. Reading comprehension is enhanced when you are able to connect new information with prior knowledge and emotion.

> Examples: Discuss text to text, text to self and text to world. Describe similarities between text and events in your town right now. How did you connect with ___ part of the book?

**Monitoring Comprehension:** when you reflect on and/or assess understanding while reading the text, active reading, active reading strategies, etc. Examples that help are rereading, taking notes in margin, and asking clarifying questions.

> Examples: Is this making sense? Should I reread this paragraph? Do you understand why the character did that?

***Visualization:*** can deepen understanding, asks to create and describe an image(s) in their mind: can be of a place, character, or event, using all 5 senses help. This also helps with recall.

    Examples: What does the character look like in this chapter? Describe the scene at the end of the page.

***Summarizing:*** what do you understand from the text, what are the most important ideas, a good summary includes the main idea and the key details that support the main idea.

    Examples: SWBST: Somebody, Wanted, But, So, Then. What are the key details to this chapter?

***Information Transfer:*** information that can be categorized, usually in a table format.

    Examples: True/False, Cause and Effect, Problems and Solutions, Before/After, Similarities/Differences, Actions/Reasons, Feelings/Actions, Advantages/Disadvantages

***Vocabulary in Context:*** questioning/analyzing vocabulary word(s) or phrase(s) in a text.

    Examples: What are two adjectives that describe ___? What does this word/phrase mean?

***Applied Vocabulary:*** must analyze vocabulary, use their own words to describe parts of the text such as a situation or character.

> Examples: How will you describe the setting in the first chapter? What words can you use to describe this character?

***Reflection:*** personal thoughts about something that happened or someone in the text.

> Examples: The character learned a lesson. Can you think of a time you learned a similar lesson? How did you handle the situation?

# READING COMPREHENSION QUESTIONS

**Introduction:**

In the introduction we read, "Don't put things where they don't belong." Mrs. Phillips said sternly, "everything has its own place." Tell me why you think LilyAnn's teacher would tell her that? Should LilyAnn listen to that advice? Why or Why not?

_____
_____
_____


Do you think LilyAnn should listen to the teacher's advice? Why or Why not?

_____
_____
_____


**Chapter 1:**

Reflect on LilyAnn's rule: Be Kind. How do you think this will shape the book? *(reflection)*

_____
_____
_____

## Chapter 2:

What can you infer LilyAnn was going to do when she says, "I made a quick decision. I glanced around the classroom to make sure no one was looking at me"? *(inferencing)*

_____
_____
_____

Why is LilyAnn twisting her hands into pretzels? *(inferencing)*

_____
_____
_____

## Chapter 3:

Why did LilyAnn's mom tell LilyAnn it's not polite to say, "only losers should be allowed to move on after a loss"? *(factual)*

_____
_____
_____

What happened after the Bulldog Divas lost their first tournament game? *(sequencing)*

_____
_____
_____

Have you ever been in a similar situation? Explain. *(making connections)*

_____
_____
_____

**Chapter 4:**

LilyAnn moved out of state: she had a new school, new teachers, new friends and new problems. What might happen with all LilyAnn's new things in her life? *(predicting)*

_____
_____
_____

What does stereotype mean? *(vocabulary in context)*

_____
_____
_____

What does self-confidence mean? *(vocabulary in context)*

_____
_____
_____

How do you think the girl in LilyAnn's class was feeling when she responded to LilyAnn by stuttering softly, "Thhaaannnnkkk yoouuuu?" *(inferencing)*

_____
_____
_____


**Chapter 5:**

Why did LilyAnn say teachers were trying to be scary when they said, "just wait 'til you get into middle school." *(inferencing)*

_____
_____
_____


How can you connect with the 5 questions that are asked in the chapter when LilyAnn mentions trying to find who you really are in 5th grade? *(making connections)*

_____
_____
_____


What 3 things does LilyAnn's #7 rule say is hard in life? *(factual)*

_____
_____
_____

## Chapter 5: Part 2

What does clique mean? Put it in a sentence. *(vocabulary in context)*

_____
_____
_____

What 3 things happened after the two girls who had been staring at LilyAnn and her friends glided over to them? *(sequencing)*

_____
_____
_____

Does this make sense to you: "I took a deep breath and started to slowly turn all the way around to face my largest mirrors, the faces of Mae and Jordan?" Explain. *(monitoring comprehension)*

_____
_____
_____

Can you describe what the #8 lesson might look like? What does it mean? *(visualization & summarizing)*

_____
_____
_____

## Chapter 6:

How does LilyAnn's goals connect with you or someone you know? *(making connections)*

_____
_____
_____


What does reputation mean? *(vocabulary in context)*

_____
_____
_____


What are 3 actions/responses you can list from chapter 6? *(actions/reasons: informational transfer)*

_____
_____
_____


What was the effect of LilyAnn not getting on the bus? *(cause/effect: informational transfer)*

_____
_____
_____


Why does LilyAnn feel guilty? *(inferencing)*

_____
_____
_____

**Chapter 7:**

What does Charlotte mean when she says, "let's start to mingle"? *(vocabulary in context & inferencing)*

_____
_____
_____


How would you describe the setting when they are walking into school on day one? *(visualization & applied vocabulary)*

_____
_____
_____


Why are LilyAnn's hands starting to sweat? Can you relate to that feeling? If so, when and why? *(inferencing & making connections)*

_____
_____
_____


LilyAnn asks, "who am I becoming?" after she put make-up on at her locker. Who do you think she'll become? *(predicting)*

_____
_____
_____

Why do you think she is suddenly not having fun anymore at the end of the chapter? *(predicting)*

_____
_____
_____


**Chapter 8:**

What happens after LilyAnn opens the cafeteria doors? *(sequencing)*

_____
_____
_____


Why do you think LilyAnn chose to sit with Mae and Jordan at lunch? *(cause/effect: informational transfer)*

_____
_____
_____


LilyAnn mentions why she lied about hearing them yell her name as the bus comes. Why? *(factual)*

_____
_____
_____

Why isn't LilyAnn going to make everyone happy in the lunchroom? *(inferencing)*

_____
_____
_____


**Chapter 9:**

The first line LilyAnn says, "After lunch, I have English with Charlotte and Mae. Oh, good." Does LilyAnn really think it's good? What makes you say that? *(inferencing)*

_____
_____
_____


Describe the scene when the new girl walks into English class. *(visualizing)*

_____
_____
_____


Have you ever experienced anything like what happened in class before? Explain. *(making connections)*

_____
_____
_____

Why does Mrs. Eachus stay by the new girl's desk longer than everyone else's? *(inferencing)*

_____
_____
_____

What was the problem having PE at the end of the day? What were some of the positives/solutions she found? *(informational transfer)*

_____
_____
_____

What does discreetly mean? Why does Jessica walk into the teacher's office that way? *(vocabulary in context & inferencing)*

_____
_____
_____

What causes LilyAnn to let out a breath when she walks into PE? *(cause/effect: informational transfer)*

_____
_____
_____

Do you think LilyAnn will catch the bus home with Mae and Jordan? Why or why not? *(predicting & inferencing)*

_____
_____
_____

What were some key details from LilyAnn's first day of middle school? Can you describe the main idea of her day? *(summarizing)*

_____
_____
_____

**Chapter 10:**

LilyAnn asks if the first week of middle school is supposed to be stressful. How can you relate? Explain *(making connections)*

_____
_____
_____

What happened after Charlotte and Raegan both put their arms through LilyAnn's? *(sequencing)*

_____
_____
_____

What happens before Charlotte and Raegan go up to LilyAnn and Mae at the lunch table? *(before/after: information transfer)*

_____
_____
_____

Why was LilyAnn scared to even look at Mae and Jordan after she agreed to go with Charlotte and Raegan? *(inferencing)*

_____
_____
_____

Have you ever made a decision and followed through with it even though you knew it was the wrong decision? *(making connections)*

_____
_____
_____

LilyAnn says she's not okay with what Charlotte is saying about Jessica but she doesn't know what she's supposed to do about it. List 3 solutions you can come up with for this problem. *(problem/solution: information transfer)*

_____
_____
_____

What does LilyAnn do to try to stop Charlotte from going on about Jessica? *(factual)*

_____
_____
_____

Charlotte's party is coming up. Make 2 predictions you think will happen at the party. *(predictions)*

_____
_____
_____

**REFLECTION / RESPONSE**

Reflect on what has happened so far in the book.

Which character do you personally relate to the most? Please explain why. Use examples from the text. *(making connections)*

_____
_____
_____
_____
_____
_____
_____
_____
_____
_____

Starting a new grade and new school is hard. Can you compare her struggle with 6th grade to something you went through? If not, how would you work through the struggles she is facing? *(making connections)*

_____
_____
_____
_____
_____
_____
_____
_____

**Chapter 11:**

LilyAnn asks, "does anyone ever look perfect?" What do you think? Why? *(reflection)*

_____
_____
_____

Can you describe how she must look/feel at this moment? *(visualization & inferencing)*

_____
_____
_____

What were the 3 things on LilyAnn's new plan for the party? *(factual)*

_____
_____
_____

Why doesn't anyone tell Charlotte no when she goes over the rules of the game? *(inferencing)*

_____
_____
_____

What 2 things does LilyAnn say Mae and Jordan are to her? *(factual)*

_____
_____
_____

What 3 things does LilyAnn do after she starts dialing Mae's phone number? *(sequencing)*

_____
_____
_____

Why does Mae's eyes fill with tears? *(inferencing)*

_____
_____
_____

Describe the last scene of the chapter with Mae and Jordan. What do you think Mae and Jordan will do next? *(visualizing & predicting)*

_____
_____
_____


What do you think 3 key points are in this chapter? *(summarizing)*

_____
_____
_____


**Chapter 12:**

What are LilyAnn's 3 big points she has realized? *(factual)*

_____
_____
_____


Do all of LilyAnn's points make sense to you? *(monitoring comprehension)*

_____
_____
_____

Can you relate to 1 or more of the points LilyAnn makes? If so, how? If not, which one do you like the most? *(making connections)*

_____
_____
_____

## COWARDS AND THE FEARLESS

What are some of the similarities and differences between the cowards and the fearless people LilyAnn was describing? *(similarities/differences: information transfer)*

_____
_____
_____

List 3 adjectives to describe each of them. *(applied vocabulary)*

| COWARDS | FEARLESS |
|---------|----------|
| -       | -        |
| -       | -        |
| -       | -        |

What is a bystander? *(vocabulary in context)*

_____
_____
_____

Why does LilyAnn see herself as a bystander? *(monitoring comprehension)*

_____
_____
_____

How can you relate to either a coward, the fearless, or bystander? *(making connections)*

_____
_____
_____

When LilyAnn tells Mae, "Middle school has been so much fun. Don't you think?" there's a question in her voice they both hear. What does that mean? *(inferencing)*

_____
_____
_____

LilyAnn tells Mae she is not involved with bullying anyone. Do you think she is? Why or why not? *(monitoring comprehension)*

_____
_____
_____

What does Jessica do when she comes out of the bathroom stall in the locker room? *(sequencing)*

_____
_____
_____


Can you tell me about Jessica's character by her reaction? *(inferencing)*

_____
_____
_____


Why does LilyAnn feel bad that someone noticed she was upset even though she's not the one getting bullied? *(inferencing)*

_____
_____
_____


LilyAnn mentions she's surprised no adult has noticed what is going on with Jessica. Do you think that's common in schools? Explain why or why not. *(making connections)*

_____
_____
_____

What does LilyAnn look like in this chapter? *(visualization)*

_____
_____
_____


**Chapter 13:**

What questions did LilyAnn, Mae and Jordan ask each other when they would talk about morals, standards, and passion? *(factual)*

_____
_____
_____


Why do you think LilyAnn doesn't have the kinds of conversations with Charlotte and Raegan that she had with Mae and Jordan? *(inferencing)*

_____
_____
_____


LilyAnn says she feels like she's being the worst person she could be. Why does she say that? Have you ever felt that way? *(factual & making connections)*

_____
_____
_____

What does captivating mean? What other words could you use in the sentence where LilyAnn says 'captivating voice'? List 3 words. *(vocabulary in context)*

_____

_____

_____

What does concocting mean? Use it in a sentence. *(vocabulary in context)*

_____

_____

_____

Jessica has had a lot happen to her. Why is Jessica smiling when she's singing? *(inferencing)*

_____

_____

_____

LilyAnn often talks about having a pit in her stomach. She mentions it again in this chapter. Can you relate? Have you ever felt like you had a pit in your stomach? When and why? *(making connections)*

_____

_____

_____

What is LilyAnn's price for popularity? *(factual)*

_____
_____
_____


LilyAnn mentions the sounds of laughter fill her up. What does that mean? What "fills you up?" *(inferencing & making connections)*

_____
_____
_____


LilyAnn mentions the sounds of laughter dying as she passes Mae and Jordan and starting to hear sounds of anger, fretting, and manipulation take their place. Why does she continue to follow the negative sounds? *(inferencing)*

_____
_____
_____


How does the scene in the bedroom remind LilyAnn of scenes in the movie Mean Girl? Can you describe that scene in your own words? *(monitoring comprehension & visualization)*

_____
_____
_____

Why did LilyAnn say she got sick to her stomach? *(cause/effect: information transfer)*

_____
_____
_____

Why did the words 'social media' make LilyAnn sick to her stomach? *(inferencing)*

_____
_____
_____

**Chapter 14:**

LilyAnn says although she isn't posting the video on social media it will still be a reflection of her. Reflect on everything that has happened. Do you agree it would be or not be a reflection? *(reflection)*

_____
_____
_____

Have you ever been in her shoes where you didn't like something your friend(s) posted on social media? How did you react? *(making connections)*

_____
_____
_____

Why does LilyAnn call herself a coward? *(factual)*

_____
_____
_____

What does it mean to go viral? *(vocabulary in context)*

_____
_____
_____

What happens before LilyAnn starts to cry on her way home? *(sequencing)*

_____
_____
_____

LilyAnn tries to reason with herself. She says things like, "I was only in the bedroom with them" and "I never actually uploaded the video to social media." Do you think that'll keep her from being blamed too? Have you ever tried to reason with yourself after something? *(reflection & making connections)*

_____
_____
_____

What does LilyAnn mean when she says, "my old friends who I've neglected yet still continue to shape me"? *(monitoring comprehension)*

_____
_____
_____


**REFLECTION / RESPONSE**

Reflect on what has happened so far in the book.

Which character do you most personally relate to now? Why? Please give at least three reasons and use make sure to give text evidence. *(making connections)*

_____
_____
_____
_____
_____
_____
_____
_____
_____
_____
_____
_____
_____

How do your friends and/or family shape you into who you are today? Please give at least three ways. Do you feel you have ever helped shape someone/helped them become the person they are today? *(making connections)*

_____
_____
_____
_____
_____
_____
_____
_____
_____
_____

**Chapter 15:**

What does humanity mean? *(vocabulary in context)*

_____
_____
_____

Why does LilyAnn's humanity grow every time she hears someone say something that Charlotte and Raegan wouldn't like in the hallway? *(inferencing)*

_____
_____
_____

Can you explain what LilyAnn is saying and/or feeling in the paragraph where she is by Lucas? The paragraph starts with, "That is probably a good thing." *(monitoring comprehension)*

_____
_____
_____


What 2 things happen as Jessica walks to her seat? *(before/after: information transfer & factual)*

_____
_____
_____


As Mae and Jordan are talking to Charlotte, Raegan and LilyAnn at their lunch table LilyAnn is silent. She says she is not strong enough to respond. Can you explain what that means? *(monitoring comprehension)*

_____
_____
_____


Have you ever felt like LilyAnn did while sitting at the lunch table? *(making connections)*

_____
_____
_____

What does sarcasm mean? Where and how is it used in this chapter? *(vocabulary in context & applied vocabulary)*

_____

_____

_____


LilyAnn finally tries to get Charlotte and Raegan to think about what they are doing and if they should continue. How did Charlotte react? Do you think she did enough, tried hard enough? (factual & reflection)

_____

_____

_____


What do you think the matching Goodwill outfits will look like? How will people react? *(predicting)*

_____

_____

_____


**Chapter 16:**

How does LilyAnn look in her Goodwill outfit? *(visualization)*

_____

_____

_____

What causes LilyAnn to talk fast to her mom when she comes into her bedroom? *(cause/effect: information transfer)*

_____
_____
_____

Why does LilyAnn's mom tell her she'd like LilyAnn to open her closet and read her lessons? *(inference)*

_____
_____
_____

Why did lesson #8 have the biggest impact on LilyAnn? Which do you think should have had the biggest impact on her? Why? *(reflection)*

_____
_____
_____

What does LilyAnn mean when she says she needs to be the square peg amongst all the circle holes that have been surrounding her? *(monitoring comprehension)*

_____
_____
_____

What are some key points of LilyAnn's 4th column, the square pegs? *(summarizing)*

_____
_____
_____


What words can you use to describe a "square peg"? List at least 5 words. *(applied vocabulary)*

_____
_____
_____


What does empowered mean? Have you ever felt empowered? *(vocabulary in context and reflection)*

_____
_____
_____


What was the effect of LilyAnn calling Mae and asking her to listen? *(cause/effect: information transfer)*

_____
_____
_____

What do you think Mae is thinking when she doesn't answer LilyAnn right away after LilyAnn asked for help? *(inferencing)*

_____
_____
_____


**Chapter 17:**

How would you respond/act if one of your friends explained all the things they were a part of like LilyAnn did that morning in her room? *(making connections)*

_____
_____
_____


Why does the outfit LilyAnn put on that morning make her feel more like her than she has in the past few months? *(inferencing)*

_____
_____
_____


What does it mean when LilyAnn says this was a start to making up with her friends; that it was her coming home? *(vocabulary in context & monitoring comprehension)*

_____
_____
_____

Why doesn't LilyAnn just run past Lucas after she ran into him in the hallway? Why do you think she tells him what she's doing and then waits for a response? *(inferencing)*

_____
_____
_____

What are 3 things Lucas says that lets LilyAnn know he is a good person? *(factual)*

_____
_____
_____

LilyAnn asks why Lucas agrees to help her. He said, "it is the right thing to do. If you can do it, then so can I." What column do you think Lucas was in before that morning? What column do you think he is in now? *(inferencing & reflection)*

_____
_____
_____

List 3 things that happen from the time LilyAnn and Mae walk into the choir room to the time they actually start talking. *(sequencing)*

_____
_____
_____

**Chapter 18:**

What does "there is no glory in being a bystander" mean? *(vocabulary in context & monitoring comprehension)*

_____
_____
_____

What does the picture of Charlotte and Raegan's mouth actually hanging wide open look like? Describe it as you see it in your mind. *(visualization)*

_____
_____
_____

What happens after LilyAnn declares 'if she has to pick being friends with them or standing up for people, she's going to stand up for people'? *(sequencing)*

_____
_____
_____

What are 2 things that happen before Raegan hits play on the phone? What are 2 things that happen after? *(sequencing)*

_____
_____
_____

What made LilyAnn stand up to Charlotte and Raegan in the hallway? *(monitoring comprehension)*

_____
_____
_____

**Chapter 19:**

List 2 reasons why LilyAnn goes to the principal's office? *(factual)*

_____
_____
_____

What were some key ideas LilyAnn thought about while sitting, waiting to talk to the principal? *(summarizing)*

_____
_____
_____

What are the 3 reasons LilyAnn picks the most uncomfortable chair to sit in when talking to the principal? *(factual)*

_____
_____
_____

LilyAnn explains a lot to the principal. List at least 5 of them in the order she explained them to him. *(sequencing)*

_____
_____
_____


Reflect on all LilyAnn has said. What do you think was the most important thing she told the principal and why? *(reflection)*

_____
_____
_____


What are 2 reasons the principal apologizes to LilyAnn? Which do you think is the most important reason? Why? *(factual & monitoring comprehension)*

_____
_____
_____


Why do you think LilyAnn cries when the principal apologizes? *(inferencing)*

_____
_____
_____

What does it mean if something is student driven? *(vocabulary in context)*

_____
_____
_____


**Chapter 20:**

When LilyAnn runs into Lucas and JR on her way to math, JR seems upset with her. Do you think he was upset? Why or why not? *(inferencing)*

_____
_____
_____


Explain the scene where the notes fall out of LilyAnn's locker. Why was it so impactful? *(inferencing & monitoring comprehension)*

_____
_____
_____


What do you think LilyAnn meant when she said she knew right then her part in all of this was going to have to go far beyond her stunt that day? *(inferencing)*

_____
_____
_____

**Chapter 21:**

Think about you, your fears and strengths. Would you be able to do what LilyAnn did on the loudspeaker? *(reflection)*

_____
_____
_____

Would you be able to do what Jessica did on the loudspeaker? (reflection)

_____
_____
_____

Analyze: what do you think the William Shakespeare quote LilyAnn uses means to you? 'It is not in the stars to hold our destiny but in ourselves.' *(analyzing & making connections)*

_____
_____
_____

**Chapter 22:**

What is a legacy? *(vocabulary in context)*

_____
_____
_____

What is your opinion of their choice for lesson #9? *(reflection)*

_____
_____
_____


Do you think starting positive social media accounts for their middle school is a good idea? Why or why not? *(reflection)*

_____
_____
_____


What do you think Charlotte means when she says this has gone far enough? *(inferencing)*

_____
_____
_____


Charlotte asks LilyAnn why she was doing all of this since they weren't being mean to her. She said LilyAnn's life was great. What wasn't Charlotte understanding? *(inferencing)*

_____
_____
_____

An 8th grade girl, Payton, praises LilyAnn for the idea. She loves it. What do you think Charlotte will feel/think after she processes that? (inferencing)

_____
_____
_____


Lucas tells LilyAnn she is a hero. What do you define a hero as? *(vocabulary in context)*

_____
_____
_____


Explain how you see their new table at lunch. Use adjectives in your description. *(visualization & vocabulary)*

_____
_____
_____


**Chapter 23:**

What are your thoughts on her last lesson, lesson #10? *(reflection)*

_____
_____
_____

What memory/event do you reflect on when you start to doubt yourself in any way? *(making connections & reflection)*

_____
_____
_____

In your opinion, what is the biggest impact/effect on the reader when Jessica's mom comes up to LilyAnn at the musical? *(reflection & inferencing)*

_____
_____
_____

Jessica's mom mentions that she feels LilyAnn gave her a new life. What do you think she means? *(inferencing)*

_____
_____
_____

Explain the importance of Charlotte's social media post. How does this help show her character development? *(monitoring comprehension)*

_____
_____
_____

## REFLECTION / RESPONSE

Reflect on what has happened so far in the book.

How do you inspire change and positivity? *(reflection)*

What can you (and your friends) do to help your school be more positive and/or help others? *(reflection)*

_____
_____
_____
_____
_____
_____
_____
_____
_____
_____

Who was your favorite character? Explain why. How did that character develop throughout the book? *(reflection & making connections)*

_____
_____
_____
_____
_____
_____
_____
_____
_____
_____

# IMPORTANCE OF READING STRATEGIES BEFORE, DURING AND AFTER READING

**BEFORE READING:**

- Increases comprehension
- Helps students access their prior knowledge
- Helps the students to engage in the text they are about to read

**DURING READING:**

- Ensures being able to monitor student's comprehension
- Encourages active reading and engagement with the text
- Increases active reading
- Improves vocabulary usage

**AFTER READING:**

- Increases ability to analyze and discuss text
- Builds student's overall reading comprehension
- Helps student's growth in analyzing and summarizing

# QUESTIONS TO ASK YOUR STUDENT BEFORE, DURING AND AFTER READING

## Before Reading *Square Peg*:

### At the beginning of Square Pegs:

What clues does the title "Square Peg" give you about what the book will be about? *(inferencing)*

What do you think the characters will be like? Why? *(inferencing)*

What do you think the book will be about? Why do you think that? *(predicting)*

Explain what the characters might be like in this book? *(predicting)*

Does the topic of the book remind you of anything you already know about or have done? *(making connections)*

Do you connect to the book description that is on the back in any way? *(making connections)*

What questions would you like to ask the author of *Square Peg* before we get started? *(monitoring comprehension)*

Are there any questions (after students look through the book)? *(monitoring comprehension)*

**When continuing *Square Peg* after a break:**

What has happened so far? *(summarizing)*

What do you think will happen next? Why? *(predicting)*

Do you have any questions so far? *(monitoring comprehension)*

Was there a part we should reread before continuing? *(monitoring comprehension)*

What notes have you taken so far? *(monitoring comprehension)*

Can you list three things that has happened in order during the last chapter we read? *(sequencing)*

# QUESTIONS TO ASK YOUR STUDENT BEFORE, DURING AND AFTER READING

## During Reading *Square Peg*:

What do you think will happen next? Why? *(predicting)*

How do you think the character will handle this situation? *(predicting)*

Which character do you think will have to overcome an obstacle? *(predicting)*

**Text to Text**

Does what happened remind you of something you have read before? *(monitoring comprehension)*

How does this character relate to others you have read about before? *(monitoring comprehension)*

**Text to Self**

Is there a character you have been able to relate to? If so, why? If not, why not? *(monitoring comprehension)*

Has anything like this ever happened to you? *(monitoring comprehension)*

How are you alike/different from this character? *(monitoring comprehension)*

**Text to World**

Have you ever met someone like this character before? *(monitoring comprehension)*

Does this situation remind you of anything that is happening, or has happened in the world? How does it relate? *(monitoring comprehension)*

What does the setting look like in your mind? *(visualizing)*

What does this character look like in your mind? *(visualizing)*

What pictures were in your mind as you have been reading this part? *(visualizing)*

Tell me what you were imagining in your remind as you read that page? *(visualizing)*

What were some cause and effect relationships you read so far? *(information transfer)*

What happened before ___ happened? *(information transfer)*

What are some of the similarities between the characters we just read? *(information transfer)*

What were some of the problems and solutions in the last chapter? *(information transfer)*

What were the 3 most important things you read today, in order of how they happened? *(sequencing)*

What are 3 things the character just did? *(sequencing)*

## Assist with self-monitoring

What questions do we have after reading this section? *(monitoring comprehension)*

Is there anything you are wondering about right now? *(monitoring comprehension)*

Did you highlight anything from the last chapter? *(monitoring comprehension)*

Why was the character sad/happy/confused? What gives you that impression? *(inferencing)*

What can you conclude about ___? *(inferencing)*

What is most likely true about ___? *(inferencing)*

Can you put what you've read in your own words? *(summarizing)*

What are 3 key points from what you read today? *(summarizing)*

What was the main idea of what you read yesterday? *(summarizing)*

# QUESTIONS TO ASK YOUR STUDENT BEFORE, DURING AND AFTER READING

## After Reading *Square Peg*:

**Text to Text**

Compare what you read today to a different piece of text you previously read. *(monitoring comprehension)*

How is this similar to other books you have read? *(monitoring comprehension)*

**Text to Self**

Can you relate to the character in the book? *(monitoring comprehension)*

Does anything in the story remind you of your life? *(monitoring comprehension)*

**Text to World**

How did the ending of the book remind you of something going on in the world? *(monitoring comprehension)*

What does the ending of the book look like in your mind? *(visualizing)*

How do you describe what the character does at the end of the book? *(visualizing)*

What pictures were in your mind when you read the ending? *(visualizing)*

What were some cause and effect relationships in what we read? *(information transfer)*

What are some of the similarities and differences between the beginning and the ending of the book? *(information transfer)*

What were some of the problems and solutions the characters faced throughout the book? *(information transfer)*

What were the 5 most important things you read in the book, in order of how they happened? *(sequencing)*

What are 3 things that happened in the last chapter? *(sequencing)*

Can you explain the importance of the character's growth in the book? *(monitoring comprehension)*

Let's talk about what you annotated while reading the last two chapters. *(monitoring comprehension)*

How do you know the character will not regret his final decision? *(inferencing)*

What do you think the author wanted you to learn by the end of the book? *(inferencing)*

Explain why you think the book ended the way it did? *(inferencing)*

Can you put what you've read in your own words? *(summarizing)*

What are 5 key points from the book? *(summarizing)*

What was the main idea of the book? *(summarizing)*

Square Peg

# You are a square peg!

www. educ8collabor8.com